"Kent Hickey is one of the funniest and most spiritual people i know. In this book, Kent has chosen a variety of Bible stories and brought them to life by providing context, Ignatian imagination, and thoughtful reflection. He then asks us to ponder questions pertinent to our times. Kent challenges us to look both within our lives and at moral dilemmas and Christian social teaching. I laughed out loud and cried a few times. It is a must read."

—Carolyn Becic,
President, St. Andrew Nativity School, Portland, Oregon

"Kent does a wonderful job of connecting seemingly distant scripture passages with our current world and then challenging us to consider how to make the message of each passage personal. What a great way to grow closer to God. *40 Days with God* invites and challenges us to discover our innermost selves."

—Dr. Matt Barmore,
Director, Ignatian Spirituality Center, Seattle

"Kent Hickey has a wonderful ability to make sense, motivate, and console. I strongly recommend this book to people of all ages."

—Rev. Eddie Reese, SJ,
President, St. Ignatius College Preparatory School, San Francisco

"This book is full of references to contemporary movies, literature, and current events. These connections allow each of us to find God in the ordinary events of daily life in ways that will surprise us and heighten our awareness of the movements of God's spirit."

—Cindy Reopelle,
Principal, Gonzaga Preparatory School, Spokane, Washington

Time Out to Journey through the Bible

40 DAYS
WITH GOD

KENT HICKEY

PARACLETE PRESS
BREWSTER, MASSACHUSETTS

2021 First Printing
40 Days with God: Time Out to Journey Through the Bible
Copyright © 2021 by Kent Hickey | ISBN 978-1-64060-604-3

The Paraclete Press name and logo (dove on cross) are trademarks of Paraclete Press.

Library of Congress Cataloging-in-Publication Data
Names: Hickey, Kent P., author.
Title: 40 days with God : time out to journey through the Bible / Kent
   Hickey.
Other titles: Forty days with God
Description: Brewster, Massachusetts : Paraclete Press, 2021. | Summary:
   "Be with God for a short time and in tight spaces; an opportunity to
   carve out God-space and God-time, a pilgrimage with God, toward God"–
   Provided by publisher.
Identifiers: LCCN 2020044736 (print) | LCCN 2020044737 (ebook) | ISBN
   9781640606043 | ISBN 9781640606050 (epub) | ISBN 9781640606067 (pdf)
Subjects: LCSH: Bible–Meditations.
Classification: LCC BS491.5 .H53 2021 (print) | LCC BS491.5 (ebook) | DDC
   242/.5–dc23
LC record available at https://lccn.loc.gov/2020044736
LC ebook record available at https://lccn.loc.gov/2020044737

10 9 8 7 6 5 4 3 2 1
Published by Paraclete Press | Brewster, Massachusetts | www.paracletepress.com
Printed in the United States of America

To My Mother and Father

Contents

Introduction

40 appears in the Bible over 100 times. Noah got rained on 40 days and nights; the Israelites wandered in the wilderness for 40 years; Jesus went into the desert to pray for 40 days after he was baptized. Some biblical scholars theorize that 40 represents a time of trial and testing; others suggest that it refers to a long time. I think it simply means enough time to be with God.

How much time is enough for us to be with God? That depends. For students at our school who go on a four-day retreat called Kairos ("God's time"), those four days are enough for them to feel how different that time is from ordinary time. For me, eight days on a silent retreat was enough time to sense the presence of God, especially as we opened each prayer session with, "God, this time is my gift to you." Throughout the Christian world, the 40 days set aside for Lent are thought to be enough time to prepare for the Sacred Triduum.

Enough time is the amount of time it takes to be in God time.

Finding enough time to be with God, however, is only half of the equation. To journey with God, we also need to find enough space. In the Bible, those who spent a long time being with God were usually in deserted places. Most of us, however, live our lives in spaces that are anything but deserted—homes, offices, schools, cars, shopping centers, gyms. Even in distracting places, however, we can carve out enough room to be with God.

In my years coaching soccer, I would often talk to players about time and space. Players need both to do the things they want to do with the ball, especially in front of the goal. If a player gets the ball in open space, opponents quickly converge, bottling up the player. Time is short and space is tight. Players need to acknowledge this reality but need not surrender to it. What is within a player's control is what she decides to do within that reality.

This book is about being with God in short time and tight spaces. The journey is taken through and with the Bible, 40 reflections based upon 40 passages from Scripture. Except for the final four chapters, the reflections are ordered in the sequence of their appearance in the Bible, starting with Genesis and ending with Revelation. The reflections can be read on their own, or with a Bible as a companion for deeper immersion into the passages. Regardless of how they are used, each reflection is designed to keep in mind a saying once popular in the rural South: "Let me sit with that."

Where and when to sit with these reflections? Within the rhythm of daily life. Try, for example, reading a reflection over a cup of coffee in the morning and then sitting with it during a commute. That's a way to fill those times—in the car, on the bus, riding a bike—with God. That makes those spaces God-spaces and those times God-times. In doing so, we make our daily journeys more like pilgrimages. With God, toward God.

40 DAYS
WITH GOD

BREEZY DAYS

*When they heard the sound of the LORD God walking about
in the garden at the breezy time of day,
the man and his wife hid themselves from the LORD God
among the trees of the garden.* —**Genesis 3:8**

I believe that we can "find God in all things," as the Ignatian saying goes. I just don't spend a lot of time looking. I have my reasons, one of them being that if I try to find God it might make it easier for God to find me. I am often very different from the "very good" being God created, a source of embarrassment for me. I'm not sure that I want to be found.

We are, all of us, very good. It's right there in the first creation story in Genesis, the one attributed to the anonymous writer that scholars refer to as the Priestly source. The Priestly author prized order, and that is reflected in the consistent pattern of days in his creation story. Key to that pattern was that God saw good in creation every day. This was especially true after God created humans, that final day when "God looked at everything he had made, and he found it very good" (Gen. 1:31).

The Priestly creation story is followed by a completely different creation story, one written by another anonymous author, designated as the "Yahwist" by scholars. God created goodness here too—in the forms of Adam and Eve. That pure goodness didn't last long though, as symbolized by their decision to eat fruit from the forbidden tree. Later, when Adam and Eve heard God walking about in the Garden of Eden, they hid themselves behind a tree. They knew that God was looking for them, and they had no desire to be found, given how embarrassed (naked) they were after what they had done.

Hiding behind a tree when God is looking for me is often where I find myself. Many types of trees offer good cover— busy-ness, ego, sloth. Usually, though, the tree is of the "I'm not worthy" variety. That feeling of nakedness before God can come from any number of lowly interactions during the day, including the beginning of the day. I am struck, for example, by how often I eat forbidden fruit during my morning commute.

How low can I go? On my drive to work, I sometimes get stuck behind a small yellow bus that is picking up a child with special needs. The delay (because the process seems so inefficient to me) often leads me to curse under my breath. On one particularly grace-filled morning, however, I found myself transported by this sight: after the mother had placed her child in the bus, I was mesmerized by the hand of the father as he waved back and forth to his child from the curb. Peace settled into my heart in this very good moment . . . until the guy in the car in front of me honked his horn and flipped off the family. I was then reminded of the many mornings when in my heart I had flipped that same finger at that family.

One would think that I am better when I ride my bike to work instead of driving. If so, one would think wrong. Biking in Seattle brings its own flip-off opportunities. I recall one especially bad day when my fellow bike commuters were particularly vexing, a lot of erratic riding and jostling. I was even cut off by some guy wearing disturbingly small, skin-tight bike shorts. I yelled at the guy, "That's a crime, man. A crime against nature!" (I may or may not have said "man.")

Right after that, I came upon a group of riders that slowed me down, all of them wearing shirts that read on the back, "Probably too old to be doing this." I thought that this was likely true as I finally started to pass them, annoyed expression firmly in place and preparing to flip a mental middle finger as I went by. Instead—to my surprise—as each of them smiled and waved at me, I found myself smiling and waving back to each of them.

Cringe-worthy moments like these pop into my head when I pray at the end of the day, and often a quotation from St. Ignatius follows: "I am an obstacle to myself." When feeling this way, I am more inclined to put up obstacles between myself and God, hiding behind a tree after the embarrassment of (once again) eating forbidden fruit. I don't want to look for God much at those times, and I certainly have no desire to be found.

What helps draw me out of hiding is the image that the Yahwist drew of God walking about in the Garden during the breezy time of day. I imagine God taking that walk every day, looking for Adam and Eve so that they could all walk together. Yes, their eating fruit from that tree hurt God, but perhaps their hiding hurt even more. It is the same with us when we find reasons to hide behind trees so that we won't be found. God doesn't care about any of those reasons, especially the I'm-not-worthy ones. What God does care about is us.

Does God still look for us? Yes. Every day. Feel the breeze from the gentle waving of a father's hand to his beloved child, and the cool waves of octogenarian bike riders. It's in those moments, and so many others, that God is looking for us, hoping that we'll let ourselves be found.

{ *What does it feel like to walk with God during the breezy time of day? Why hide?*

THE CROUCHER

*So the L*ORD *said to Cain: "Why are you resentful and crestfallen? If you do well, you can hold up your head; but if not,
sin is a demon lurking at the door: his urge is toward you,
yet you can be his master."* —**Genesis 4:6–7 (NAB)**

The story is well known. Cain and Abel each gave offerings
to God. Abel gave his best; Cain apparently didn't. Cain
became resentful, lured Abel into a field, and murdered him. It's
a big leap from feeling bad about a rejected gift to killing your
brother. What explains it? We have some clues in the text.

First, there is the quality of the gifts. Abel's gift was one of
the "best" firstlings of his flock. There is no qualitative word
attached to Cain's gift—"from the fruit of the soil." It's reasonable to
infer from the lack of a descriptor—and from what we know about
Cain—that his offering was likely a meager one, given with tight
fists. Cain didn't have a generous heart, and his gift (maybe rotten
fruit) reflected that.

God rejected Cain's gift, but tried to soothe Cain's hurt
feelings with a little pep talk: *If you do well . . . because you just
once again didn't do well . . . you can hold up your head. Earn it;
stop whining.* That's not how Cain saw it, though. The rejection
was an injustice, yet another injury in a long line inflicted by his

calculating brother. Cain needed someone to blame, because, as resentful people are inclined to do, he refused to look honestly within himself.

Finally, there is God's warning: *A demon is lurking at your door, and this demon wants you bad. But I know you can overcome it, Cain, if only you would try!* Cain's demon was resentment, a feeling he'd likely grown attached to over the years. His desire to have that feeling was stronger than his desire to master it, so he caved into it. At that point, murder came easily to Cain. Hands follow the heart.

The Hebrew for "demon" is "croucher." Evil crouches at the door of every heart, lurking, waiting for an opening. But, the croucher can't enter without being let in. That seems simple enough—just master the evil; keep the croucher outside. The problem is that the croucher is very attractive, and it can morph into whatever we are most attracted to. For Cain, it was resentment. For the rest of us . . .

I remember playing in a softball game when I lived in Milwaukee many years ago. The game was delayed because police cars and ambulances had converged outside a nearby apartment building. We found out later what all the commotion was about. Jeffrey Dahmer had been arrested and the contents of his freezer—human body parts—were carted from his apartment.

Monstrous, to be sure. But inhuman? That's another scary part of the story.

Dahmer's defense attorney and the prosecuting attorney were both graduates of the high school where I was teaching. After the trial ended, we invited the attorneys to speak with our senior class. The attorneys shared the same disturbing conclusion each had drawn about Dahmer—that he was in most ways like the rest of us. In fact, he possessed many positive qualities: polite, thoughtful, and intelligent. What he knew about himself was that he had a perverse attraction to murder and engaging in deeply disturbing acts with the body. He didn't want to be that way, and so he tried to master the temptation. That went on for years. At one point, however, he began letting those desires into his heart. His horrific crimes followed shortly thereafter.

Thankfully, that is an extreme example, but it's also an illustrative one. All of us have demons crouching at the door that yearn to master us. They often seem harmless. Who is to fault Cain, for example, for feeling some resentment when what he had offered as a gift was rejected? How harmful can hurt feelings be? Very harmful if they morph into the kind of feeling that ends in murder.

And so it is with each and every one of us. Letting the croucher through the door can lead to murder, likely in our hearts or words, but murder, nonetheless. Even more worrisome, those demons can be anything, even healthy desires that devolve into unhealthy obsessions: pride to arrogance; passion to anger; loving to possessing. It is, as C. S. Lewis said, "the subtlest of snares."

What to do? Look to God's pep talk to Cain—the croucher can be mastered if we do well. Doing well here means following Abel's example: keeping our hearts filled with goodness, generosity, and the desire to do our best in God's service. Hearts full of those things have less room for hateful things, leaving little space for the croucher to enter and take up residence.

What is crouching at the door of my heart?

day three
ACT OF GOD

*"When I bring clouds over the earth, and the bow appears
in the clouds, I will remember the covenant I have made
between me and you and every living creature . . .—so that
the waters will never again become a flood to destroy every
mortal being."* **—Genesis 9:14–15**

As a kid growing up during the Cold War, I feared—we all feared—the threat of nuclear war. To combat this fear, we were required to practice nuclear fallout drills at school, usually by hiding under our desks. It was during one such drill, I think in fifth grade, that an incorrigible soul asked from under his desk, "Will this really keep us safe from a nuclear bomb?" Our teacher, Sister Alfred, was not pleased.

Fear of chaos is ingrained in the human psyche. While the form may change—nuclear war, 9/11, school shootings, pandemic—what remains the same is the overwhelming anxiety that chaos stirs up inside. What helps, even if it's illusory, is an explanation for the chaos or a way to exert some control over its impact. That's why that fifth grader's question was so unnerving. We had nothing, and Sister Alfred knew it. Ducking under desks offered no protection from being burnt to a crisp; she just wanted us to feel that it could.

For our biblical ancestors, chaos took the form of uncontrollable, raging waters. The Priestly writer, author of the first creation story, described how God brought order out of chaos by creating a dome in the sky that divided the water, and then pooled the water below into a single basin so that dry land would emerge (Gen. 1:6–10). God went on to complete creation in six days and rested on the seventh. But creation didn't pan out as planned. As humans multiplied, they also became increasingly evil, a big mistake. God took corrective action by bringing chaos back: The floodgates in the dome were opened and waters once again covered the earth, drowning most of humanity (Gen. 7–8).

Chaos took the form of flood waters because the early Hebrew people, like their Mesopotamian neighbors, retained the memory of a prehistoric cataclysmic flood. The oldest known account of that great flood is found in the Epic of Gilgamesh, a Sumerian myth that predates Genesis. The early Hebrews almost certainly took their story from that story. Both include a big boat that saved a family from the flood and birds that were released until one found dry land and didn't return. The Genesis story is very different from the Epic of Gilgamesh, however, in the most important way: what it tells us about who God is and who God is not, especially when it comes to chaos.

Ancient peoples had the same fear of chaos that we have, and the same desire for some semblance of order. They found it by pinning the blame for chaos on the gods, and they accepted whatever the gods hurled at them, even if their reasons were stupid. In the Epic of Gilgamesh, for example, the floodgates were opened because humans were just too loud, and one god wanted to shut them up (forever). That makes no sense—although neither does hiding under desks to protect from nuclear attack.

We have advanced far beyond those near-Neanderthal Mesopotamians, have we not? That's up for debate. When a tornado rolls through the Plains, just missing one town while destroying another, someone interviewed on the news is sure to say, "Guess it was the will of God." That kind of thinking is even ingrained in our legal system. When insurance companies want to get out from under a claim for damages caused by an earthquake, volcanic eruption, or flood, they escape liability through the "Act of God" clause.

Even more concerning, attributing destructive chaos to God wreaks havoc on belief. It reduces God to the puniness of those ancient gods, a maniacal puppeteer with little regard for creation. Every school year I have to overcome this "God-the-manipulative-destroyer" mindset that sophomores bring to Scripture studies. On the first day of class I ask them to "draw God" and, sure enough, at least half of them come up with this bearded, angry old man holding lightning bolts. Pretty much Zeus. Try inviting teenagers to fall in love with that.

That is why when I teach the Noah flood story, I don't spend a lot of time on the flood. Yes, God did get angry and drown most of humanity, looking a lot like those Mesopotamian gods while doing so. That depiction of God, however, is drawn more from human imagination than divine inspiration. Where God's revelation of who God really is can be found at the end of the flood story.

It is here where we see the first reference to "covenant" in Hebrew Scripture, an agreement between God and God's people that reaffirms God's feelings for us when we were first created: "God looked at everything he had made, and he found it very good" (Gen. 1:31). Even more, God placed a reminder of those feelings and the covenant in the clouds. Popularized as simply a rainbow, it's more than that: God put his "keshet" in the sky, his war bow. God will not aim his weapon at humanity again; it has been hung up for good. God loves us too much to do otherwise.

{ *If God cannot be found in the cause of chaos, how might God be found in its wake?*

day four
CUT UP

*Circumcise the flesh of your foreskin. That will be the sign of
the covenant between me and you.* —**Genesis 17:11**

There's just no getting around circumcision in the Bible. It pops
up everywhere, a source of discomfort and even anxiety for
high school religion teachers.

In my early teaching years, I navigated circumcision passages
by skirting around them. I usually muttered something about it
being a medical procedure and then moved on before students
had time to ask questions.

In later, more confident years, I met circumcision head on:
"It was a religious ritual performed shortly after the birth of a
Jewish male that involved cutting away the foreskin of the penis."
I then paused for questions, knowing that students wanted to
flee from this topic as quickly as possible. Even those girls who
consistently (and rightfully) challenged the teachings of the
Bible because of its constant male-first emphasis fell mute, as if
to say, "Ok, they can have this one."

Once—and only once—did a student break the silence with a
question. It was one word: "Why?"

I answered by describing how, from Abraham through the
generations thereafter, circumcision was the sign of the

Covenant between God and God's people. In the early years, circumcision also set Israel apart from its neighbors (Canaanites, Philistines, etc.) and, later, it distinguished Jews from their conquerors, especially the Greeks and Romans. The world was divided between the circumcised and uncircumcised.

I also explained that, as described in the Acts of the Apostles, circumcision was the first great controversy in the early Church. Would gentiles be required, as dictated by leaders in Jerusalem, to first become Jewish before becoming Christian (meaning get circumcised)? Or, as St. Paul believed, could gentiles become Christian without having to first become Jewish (remain uncircumcised)? Thankfully, St. Paul won out. Christianity might have died then and there if he hadn't.

The student who had asked "Why?" patiently endured my lengthy response, and then followed up with, "I still don't understand why something like circumcision was used as the sign of the Covenant." My initial thought was, "Because God has a sense of humor." But I pivoted instead to one of the best tools in the teaching toolbox—delay. "Let's explore that terrific question in our next class."

During the next class I read aloud excerpts from A. J. Jacobs's *The Year of Living Biblically*.[1] Jacobs had chronicled his year of following the laws set forth in the Torah (or Pentateuch, the first five books in Hebrew Scripture) as literally as possible. This included well-known laws such as the Ten Commandments, and also the obscure ones, including no mixed fibers in clothing, stoning an adulterer (with a pebble), and never sitting where his wife had sat when she was experiencing her menstrual cycle (which prompted his wife to sit on all the chairs in their apartment every day before Jacobs returned home). It's a very funny book, and very poignant. Observing all those laws so faithfully awoke within Jacobs a newfound appreciation for his Jewish faith.

Which is exactly what all these laws, when taken together, are supposed to do. Yes, we can isolate any number of laws in any faith tradition and label them as outdated and even ridiculous. But, the laws of Judaism, Christianity, Islam, etc., should be viewed as whole, not piecemeal.

On the opposite end of the spectrum, neither should these laws be viewed as the faith itself. The danger in every faith tradition is that laws get worshiped more than God. Religious laws, regardless of the faith, are not meant to be *the* faith. They exist to point us in the direction of God as we try to live faithfully.

That is exactly what the many laws in the Pentateuch, when taken together, were all about. They served as constant reminders to the Jewish people of that time (and this time) that always—every day in every way—God was present. This was especially true of the greatest law, the *Shema*, as found in Deuteronomy 6:5: "Therefore, you shall love the LORD, your God, with your whole heart, and with your whole being, and with your whole strength." How important was the *Shema*? There was also a law that required that a small box be strapped to the forehead, a tiny scroll with the words of the *Shema* placed within. Thus, the law most essential to be mindful of was literally affixed to the mind.

Strangely (at least to us today), circumcision operated the same way, although the physical nature of the act cut even deeper (so to speak). The change to the exterior (it's here where most students cringe) was to be a reminder that our relationship with God changes the interior (it's here that some of them start to get it). Without that deeper meaning, it really had no meaning.

It was the Prophet Jeremiah who best captured what circum-cision really meant: "Be circumcised for the LORD, remove the foreskins of your hearts . . ." (Jeremiah 4:4). Only the heart that is cut open can receive the Lord.

What would a circumcision of the heart require?

day five
BROTHERLY LOVE

Let the time of mourning for my father come,
so that I may kill my brother Jacob. —**Genesis 27:41**

When he was just a baby, Hercules strangled snakes that Hera had sent to attack him. Harry Potter was still in his crib when he fought off Voldemort. That kind of foreshadowing often supports wonderful story lines. One of the best of its kind is the birth account of Jacob and Esau in Genesis.

Esau was born first: "The first to emerge was reddish, and his whole body was like a hairy mantle; so they named him Esau." The key words are "red" and "hairy"—in Hebrew the name "Esau" connects to both. Picture Esau storming out of the womb as a human hairball, maybe smoking a cigar. He's wild, unsophisticated, and, as we see later, not so bright.

Jacob came out literally on the heel of Esau, grasping it as if he wanted to pull Esau back so that he could emerge from the womb first. That "grasping" is the basis for the name "Jacob." It's the key to the story line: Jacob is a climber, determined to be number one. The question is what he will do with his grasp: Will Jacob lift others up with him, or will he drag them down as he pulls himself up?

The question is answered when the story shifts to Jacob and Esau as young men. As foreshadowed in the birth scene, Jacob becomes all about Jacob. Esau, the firstborn, was entitled to a special birthright and blessing from their father, Isaac. Jacob stole both, pulling Esau back so that Jacob could come out on top.

The birthright was easy to take. Esau was a skillful hunter; Jacob "stayed among the tents." One day, Jacob made a red stew and Esau, famished after a hunt, demanded, "Let me gulp down some of that red stuff; I am famished." (There's the red again. Passion ruled Esau, and Jacob knew it.) Jacob offered the stew to Esau in exchange for the birthright. Esau agreed. "I am on the point of dying. What good is the right as firstborn to me?"

Stealing the blessing required more cunning. Isaac—old, blind, and likely of the same IQ as Esau—sent Esau to kill game for his dinner. The firstborn blessing, Isaac promised, would be given to Esau at the meal's conclusion. Jacob saw his opportunity and seized it. He prepared a dinner for Isaac that tasted like game and then, after putting animal fur on his arms and dressing in a smelly cloak, presented himself to Isaac as Esau. Isaac fell for it and gave Jacob the firstborn blessing.

Esau was enraged to the point of murder, and Jacob fled for his life, living many years thereafter exiled from his family. During those years Jacob experienced hardships, including being tricked out of a wife for a time, and those experiences changed him. Jacob became less about Jacob.

The story doesn't follow Esau during these years, but its ending indicates that he changed as well. Esau came to see in a different color than red. When Jacob returned to Esau—"bowing to the ground seven times, until he reached his brother"—Esau didn't take revenge, didn't even stand aloof expecting his brother to grovel at his feet. Instead, "Esau ran to meet him, embraced him, and flinging himself on his neck, kissed him as he wept."

The "nature vs. nurture" argument isn't much of an argument at all. Surely, we carry much of who we are in the DNA we're born with. Being a burly, red chia pet with anger management issues came naturally to Esau, just as Jacob was predisposed to ruthless social climbing. But predisposition isn't predestination. We don't have to act in the ways that come most naturally to us.

At some point Esau decided that violent passions wouldn't rule him. He chose mercy over vengeance. Jacob decided that there could be more to relationships than climbing over bodies to get to the top. He chose humility over arrogance. Emptied of some of the junk they carried within, Jacob and Esau were then free to become more than what they had been foreshadowed to be.

{ *Is there something from youth that foreshadowed anything about how you live today? Is that a welcome thing, or is it junk you would rather dispose of?*

SAME AS THE OLD BOSS

*Then Shechem appealed to Dinah's father and brothers: "Do
me this favor, and whatever you ask from me, I will give.
No matter how high you set the bridal price and gift, I will
give you whatever you ask from me; only give me the young
woman as a wife."* —**Genesis 34:11–12**

The best stories in the Pentateuch were written by the Yahwist
writer. We don't know the author's name, so she is referred
to by the name her tribe in Judea used for God, "Yahweh." (Those
who lived in the north called God "Elohim," so the author of those
passages in the Pentateuch is called the Elohist.)

The Yahwist was likely a man given the culture; however,
some scholars believe it is possible that she was a woman. Their
reasoning is not so flattering for men: Sometimes referred to as
the world's first novelist, the Yahwist wrote so masterfully and
with such depth of understanding—especially when describing
human emotions and relationships—that the level of complexity
far exceeded other writings of the time. The difference in the
writings, it's theorized, can be attributed to the fact that the writer
was different (not male).

There's no better evidence for this theory than Genesis 34.
Dinah, the daughter of Jacob, was raped by Shechem, son of

Hamor the Hivite. After the rape, Shechem told Hamor to "get me this young woman for a wife." So, Hamor met with Jacob to see if a deal could be struck. Now, this was the same Jacob who, as a young man, had tricked his brother out of both a birthright and blessing. While Jacob had grown over the years, that conniving nature remained and reared itself in Jacob's negotiations with Hamor. Jacob knew that the Hivites were both an existential threat and potential ally, so he perceived that an opportunity for a useful political alliance had presented itself. The price Jacob was willing to pay to get what he wanted was to marry his daughter off to her rapist.

Jacob's sons—"speaking with guile because their sister had been defiled"—agreed to the arrangement under the condition that all the male Hivites get circumcised. The Hivites agreed to this and, as they recovered in their tents, Jacob's sons swooped in, killed them, and looted the town. Jacob angrily confronted his sons, to which they replied, "Should our sister have been treated like a prostitute?" We don't know if Jacob answered the question.

What we do know is that, running beneath the narrative, was a question the Yahwist was asking that few wanted to hear: "Whose voice is missing?" Dinah's! She did not appear in the story after the rape. We don't know if she ever had the chance to confront her rapist (likely not), we don't know what she thought of her dad using her as a bargaining chip (likely not much), and we also don't know how she felt about being excluded from the revenge exacted upon the rapist and his men (likely left out).

We look at this story and think, "How horrible were those people in those days!" But it doesn't take a lot of honest reflection to recognize that the problem of excluded voices wasn't just a 4,000-years-ago problem. Women remain reluctant to speak out about sexual violence, fearing that their voices won't be taken seriously. And remnants remain of once common defense strategies during rape trials: painting pictures of victims who'd been given what they were asking for because of what they had worn, how much they had drunk, or how many sexual encounters they'd had.

Fortunately, we're a better society now than then. Any advances we have made, however, have been almost entirely dependent upon what voices have been heard. Where there have been bountiful female voices in board rooms, church meetings, courtrooms, legislatures, and cabinets, the results have been better, more equitable decisions in business, religion, verdicts, legislation, and the exercise of power. When those voices are missing, injustice and stupidity prevail.

The lesson of the Dinah story is one that we need to keep learning. It would be a mistake to relegate it to a bygone era. God still speaks in the words written by the Yahwist: Beware of silenced Dinahs and Jacob–Hamor pacts.

Only the most ignorant or mean-spirited person today would agree that silencing voices such as Dinah's is appropriate. But do vestiges of this bygone era remain?

day seven
40

*"Remember how for forty years now the Lord, your God, has
directed all your journeying in the desert...."*
—Deuteronomy 8:2 (NAB)

As I was about to begin a silent eight-day retreat, I texted
some of my colleagues at Jesuit schools and asked for their
prayers. One of them started a pool—When Will Hickey Crack?—
and chose Day 1 for his entry.

That looked to be the winning pick when the retreat director
described what silence would require on this retreat: no talking
(in words, glances, or gestures), no electronic devices, no
reading, no writing, no praying, and ... no thinking. The director,
a German Jesuit named Fr. Anton, told us, "It is simple, but it is
hard." He was right.

The hardest part was not thinking because, as Fr. Anton
explained, "If you are not thinking, you are dead." Awareness.
That was it and all of it. But the problem with awareness is that
it leads to thinking, which then leads to planning, etc. Vigilance
was required, remaining aware only of sounds, sights, and smells
without drifting into thinking. A constant battle for me.

I used bird sounds to snap back to awareness whenever
I drifted into thinking. Since there were a lot of birds around,

this worked well, a kind of conditioned response. Over time I started to understand what was happening inside. As I created wider space through awareness, I found myself with more room to become present to another presence.

When the Israelites fled from slavery in Egypt, it was only 200 miles to the Promised Land (Canaan), a three-week journey by foot. That three-week journey took the Israelites 40 years. "40" in the Bible, however, is never about clock time. It is about *enough* time. For the Israelites, 40 years was enough time for the spiritual transformation of a people from one that didn't know God to one that did. Jesus also had a 40 time, though his was days and nights. Jesus's 40 was enough time to prepare for public ministry after his baptism by John.

In both of those examples, the place was just as essential as the time. The Israelites wandered in the desert (the Sinai Peninsula); Jesus remained in a desert to pray and fast. Deserts provide enough deserted space to quiet distractions, to flush the disruptions inside into the surrounding silence. As we are emptied within, room is carved out for what really sustains us. For the Israelites, that was a law written into their hearts instead of one in stone. For Jesus, it was the certain knowledge of who he was, an identity so strong that Jesus could withstand the attempts of the evil one to tempt him into being who he was not.

On the silent retreat, my 40 was eight days in clock time. My desert was a quiet chapel. Both were enough time and space to hollow out room for what I really needed. It came with a single word.

Throughout most days of the retreat, we would sit with a word that Fr. Anton gave to us. One day, the word was "yes," which I imagined in the palms of my hands, slowly breathing it in and out. As the day went along, I noticed that I saw "joy" instead of "yes" in my palms. I tried to put that out of mind—that wasn't the focal word for the day. "Joy," however, kept coming back, until I finally surrendered to it and prayed "joy" with each breath. After a while—I don't know how long—I began to tremble as tears of joy streamed down my face. I was overwhelmed by the awareness of how much God loves me.

While the retreat was hard, in some ways the time after the retreat was harder. Where could I find my desert and 40 in the space and time I normally occupy? I've been disappointed by how poorly I've carried that retreat into everyday life. I feel reassured, however, whenever I become mindful of what Fr. Anton told me at the end of the retreat: "Jesus will tell you what you need to know; your desire to be with Him is enough." And even better is when I recall his final words: "Keep the joy."

{ *Where is there a desert to visit each day? When is there enough time in the day to visit it?*

day eight
FEASTING

*Then Moses went up from the plains of Moab to
Mount Nebo, the headland of Pisgah which faces
Jericho, and the LORD showed him all the land....
"This is the land which I swore to Abraham, Isaac
and Jacob that I would give to their descendants. I
have let you feast your eyes upon it,
but you shall not cross over."*
—Deuteronomy 34:1–4 (NAB)

Wouldn't you think that, for all Moses did during his life,
God would have treated him better when it ended? Look at
his resume: Moses answered God's call to free the Israelites from
slavery in Egypt. Later, while at Mount Sinai, Moses delivered
God's law to the people. (It's even called the Mosaic Law.) Then
Moses led the Israelites in the desert during their long journey
to the Promised Land, a time made even longer for Moses given
all the complaining and criticizing he endured. "He had no equal
in all the signs and wonders the LORD sent him to perform in the
land of Egypt against Pharaoh . . . and for the might and terrifying
power that Moses exhibited in the sight of all Israel" (Deut. 34:11–
12, NAB).

His reward? God denied Moses entry into the Promised Land. He died on the outside looking in.

Scripture tells us that Moses was not allowed to cross over into the Promised Land because of the sinfulness of the generation that had escaped slavery. Only the next generation would cross over, a prohibition that included Moses—"You shall not enter there either . . ." (Deut. 1:37). But that reason does not satisfy. For one, the blameless Moses was punished along with the blameworthy. More to the point, given all that he had done, didn't Moses deserve much more than what he got?

Sadly, no. There is a hard truth in Moses's harsh ending: To quote Clint Eastwood from the Western epic *Unforgiven*, "Deserves got nothing to do with it."[2] It was a fact of life for Moses—as it is for all of us—that how we live our lives has little bearing on how our lives end. Scoundrels sometimes enjoy blessed deaths; the blessed often die in tragic circumstances. Look at, for example, the thousands of good people who were bedridden and died alone during the pandemic. Life is unfair, and that includes how life ends for many of us.

There is not a lot of solace, therefore, in the "you shall not cross over" passage. However, we can find some if we dig a little deeper. It is found in the preceding phrase, "I have let you feast your eyes upon it. . . ." Maybe God didn't treat Moses so shabbily after all.

While gazing on the Promised Land, Moses could see how his efforts had brought his people closer to their goal. He feasted upon the certainty of a life meaningfully led. Equally important, Moses could see himself in those he had inspired to carry on the work: "Now Joshua, son of Nun, was filled with the spirit of wisdom, since Moses had laid his hands upon him . . ." (Deut. 34:9).

Joshua would lead the people in circles around Jericho, and the walls would come tumbling down. That was Moses's victory lap.

A life well lived doesn't depend upon how it ends. There is a poignant scene from the movie *Parenthood* that speaks to this truth. A father (Jason Robards) explains to his son (Steve Martin) what parenting means: "There is no end zone. You never cross the goal line and spike the ball and do your touchdown dance. Never."[3] What is true for parenting is also true for life. Most of us do not get to dance in the end zone. Better to celebrate, then, all that was done to inch us closer to it.

That is exactly the point of the wonderful prayer "A Future Not Our Own." It is often used when reflecting upon the unfinished business that was the life of Archbishop Oscar Romero, but it applies to all of us: "We accomplish in our lifetime only a tiny fraction of the magnificent enterprise that is God's work. Nothing we do is complete, which is another way of saying that the Kingdom always lies beyond us. . . ."

Moses did not complete his work—none of us complete our work. But doing even a tiny fraction of God's work moves us closer to the Promised Land, a vision worth feasting upon.

This use of the imagination is not as morbid as it may seem: Picture yourself upon your deathbed. As you look upon your life, what is it that you most want to feast upon?

day nine
CONSECRATED

For the boy shall be consecrated to God from the womb, until the day of his death. —**Judges 13:7 (NAB)**

The boy referenced in the reading from Judges is Samson. He was consecrated—sanctified—from the moment he was in his mother's womb. Samson was a Nazirite, from "nazir" in Hebrew, meaning that he was sacred. Samson, like all Nazirites, could not cut or shave his hair (Num. 6:5). As Samson's hair grew, so also did his strength, and Samson became the defender of the Israelites against the Philistines.

That is, until Samson started to act like a philistine. He strayed from the womb that had birthed him. The Hebrew word for faith is "Emunah," and the root of that word is "mother." As Samson drifted from his faith, he grew apart from everything that had made him special. When he caved to Delilah's charms, what really caved was his faith. Locks sheared, Samson became just another guy. He had forgotten that he'd been consecrated in the womb, a consecration that gave him faith-strength, the kind of strength that has nothing to do with being able to kill a thousand men with the jawbone of an ass.

We are all consecrated in the womb. The inherent sacredness of every human being is core to Scripture, right there at the beginning of Genesis. The human is made in God's image; God imprints on each of us. This sacredness can never be taken from us, even though we often forget that we have it. And, because we forget this about ourselves, we also forget this about others.

That forgetfulness changes culture, and not for the better. Without inherent value, each person is required to offer something of value in order to be valued. That is, only those who can bring something tangible to the table are welcome at the table. Those perceived to bring little value—those who are unborn, poor, developmentally disabled, refugees, mentally ill, elderly—fail the cost-benefit analysis.

Even more, reducing humans to commodities reduces relationships to transactions. What I will do for you depends upon what you can do for me. That kind of transactional culture reduces human beings to things, and, in so doing, desecrates (de-sanctifies) the human. Such a different culture from the biblical ideal that holds up every human as sacred, knit lovingly by God in the womb (Ps. 139:13). How would our world be different if we viewed each other as consecrated instead of as commodities? Everything would change, starting with the smallest of things.

A young man I coached many years ago visited with me after a lengthy trip abroad. He had stayed in Bali for a month and described it as the best part of his trip. I was struck by the reason he had found it so enjoyable: the Balinese always smile when encountering strangers on the street. My young friend told me that it was as if each person were saying, "I don't know you, but I think it would be good to know you." The cumulative effect of those daily interactions left him smiling more, a quiet joy having settled in.

"I don't know you, but I think it would be good to know you." That doesn't depend upon what you can do for me, since I don't even know you. All it depends upon is that I know you are a fellow human being, and that's enough to make me smile. When we get to that point, we're not viewing each other through our own eyes. Now we're seeing through God's eyes.

Pope Francis was once asked what more he could do to make the world more beautiful. He responded, "I would like to smile always." That's a remarkable answer, considering all the directions he could have taken that question. Pope Francis has also described how natural it is to smile when looking upon a baby. That's so true, even though a baby can't do anything for any of us besides being a baby.

Maybe that's what Jesus was talking about when he said that we must become like little children if we are to enter the Kingdom. When we recover our childlike spirit we also recover what deep down we know about ourselves—that we have been consecrated from the womb. What we see in ourselves we also see in others. The sacred within.

{ *Anthony De Mello, SJ, a Jesuit priest from India, once said, "Behold God, beholding you . . . and smiling." What's God smiling about?*

day ten
THE BEST
SCRIPTURE PASSAGE EVER

Ruth said, "Do not press me to go back and abandon you!
Wherever you go I will go, wherever you lodge I will lodge,
your people shall be my people, and your God, my God."
—Ruth 1:16

M oab was the last place any Israelite family would want to settle. Due to a severe famine in Israel, however, that was exactly where Naomi and her family ended up.

It was during the time of the Judges, that two-hundred-year period of tribal warfare and chaos that took place between the Israelites' entry into the Promised Land and the establishment of the monarchy under King Saul. Israel was surrounded by enemies, none more loathed than the oppressive, bullying Moabites. How much did the Israelites hate them? Included in Genesis is a description of how Moab, the original ancestor of all Moabites, was a product of a night of drunken sex between Lot and one of his daughters (Gen. 19:30–38). In Hebrew, Moab means "From my father," some biblical trash talk. It's doubtful that this origin story ever found its way into Moabite history books.

After settling in Moab, Naomi's husband died, and she was left widowed with her two sons. Fortunately, Naomi's sons found two Moabite women to marry, Orpah and Ruth. Unfortunately, the two sons then died, leaving their wives childless.

Naomi decided to return to Israel and insisted that her daughters-in-law remain in Moab: "Why come with me? Have I other sons in my womb who could become your husbands?" (Ruth 1:11). Orpah relented and remained in Moab. Ruth, however, refused to abandon Naomi.

Ruth's decision to remain with Naomi and relocate to Israel was one of the most generous recorded in the Bible. Given that a woman's worth at that time was measured by how many children she had, Ruth risked living a barren life by sticking with Naomi. And then there was Naomi herself, a name that means "pleasant," which she was not. Naomi was a constant complainer, not exactly your ideal traveling companion. Finally, there were the dim prospects that awaited Ruth as a Moabite living among Israelites. While the Mosaic Law required that the "alien who resides with you (be treated) no differently than the natives born among you" (Lev. 19:34), it wasn't likely that abundant charity would be extended to a Moabite woman in the land of Israel. The safe way to go for Ruth would have been to send Naomi on her way.

That Ruth did not choose the safe way—but instead took a holy way—is why I think this is the best Scripture passage ever. We can find all the elements of holy living in Ruth's declaration: "Wherever you go I will go, wherever you lodge I will lodge." Ruth fully, unambiguously commits to Naomi in her time of need and vulnerability. "Your people shall be my people." Ruth agrees to fully immerse herself in a community that would probably stigmatize and alienate her upon arrival. (Indeed, the Israelites would refer to her as "Ruth the Moabite.") Finally, Ruth commits to faith in a God that is completely different from Moabite gods, relying solely upon the word of her chosen family when they told her about this God.

The path to holiness is all there: love for the person, embracing community, desire to surrender to the will of God. What is more, there are no conditions attached to any of it, no wiggle room carved out so that Ruth could walk away from the promise if things went bad. Ruth declared she would do all those things, and she meant it.

Ruth's sincere conviction suggests another clear, unambiguous declaration that would be heard from the lips of another holy woman a thousand years later. They are the words spoken by Mary in response to the angel Gabriel's invitation that she give birth to Jesus: "Behold, I am the handmaid of the Lord. May it be done to me according to your word" (Lk. 1:38). No wiggle words there either.

There is an additional connection to Jesus in the story, one found in its happy conclusion. Ruth's goodness became known throughout her new hometown, Bethlehem. Included among her admirers was Boaz, a wealthy landowner, and they became husband and wife. They had a child, Obed, who had a son named Jesse (of Jesse Tree fame). His son was King David. Ruth, therefore, a member of the despised Moabite tribe, became the great-grandmother of the greatest king in Israel and, as written in the Gospel of Matthew, the ancestor of Jesus, born in Bethlehem.

{ *Is the path to holiness really as simple as love of person, community, and God?*

day eleven
DAVID'S ARMOR

Then Saul dressed David in his own tunic, putting a bronze
helmet on his head and arming him with a coat of mail.
David also fastened Saul's sword over the tunic. He walked
with difficulty, however, since he had never worn armor
before. . . . So he took them off. **—1 Samuel 17:38–39**

The Philistine Goliath taunted the Israelites across the valley that separated the two armies: "I defy the ranks of Israel today. Give me a man and let us fight together." Massive and menacing, Goliath left the Israelites "stunned and terrified." No one in the Israelite army was brave enough to accept Goliath's challenge.

This went on, morning and evening, for forty days. (Meaning a long time, which is what forty sometimes symbolizes in Scripture.) Such humiliation for the sheepish Israelites, especially their king, Saul. Hope arrived in the person of a shepherd, David, a skinny teenager fresh from tending his flock. Though a boy, David called out the Israelites for their lack of manliness: "How will the man who kills this Philistine and frees Israel from disgrace be rewarded? Who is this uncircumcised Philistine that he should insult the armies of the living God?"

What a teenager thing to do, brashly calling out adults by speaking a truth no one wanted to hear. David's boldness didn't go over well with at least one adult, his older brother: "I know your arrogance and dishonest heart. You came down to enjoy the battle!" David's response was another teenage classic: "What have I done now?—I was only talking."

Saul heard about David's talking and called for him. However, when David arrived, Saul saw only a boy, not a way out of his embarrassing dilemma: "You cannot go up against this Philistine and fight with him, for you are only a youth, while he has been a warrior from his youth." David countered by describing how he had subdued wild animals while tending his flocks: "Your servant has killed both a lion and a bear, and this uncircumcised Philistine will be as one of them, because he has insulted the armies of the living God."

It's not boasting if you can back it up. And that is just what David did, although not in the way that Saul thought he should. Saul wanted David to act like other warriors, to dress and fight like everyone else. David, though "only a youth," possessed remarkable maturity and self-awareness. He rejected Saul's sword and armor—they didn't fit him. He instead picked up five smooth stones and, with sling in hand, confronted the Philistine. David knew himself well enough to know what fit him best. He didn't try to be another Saul. David decided to be David, confident that his strengths would make him strong enough.

What followed was some epic pre-battle trash talk between Goliath and David. Each promised the other that his corpse would be providing dinner to a lot of animals that day. But David also made it clear where his real strength came from: "All this multitude, too, shall learn that it is not by sword or spear that the

LORD saves. For the battle belongs to the Lord, who shall deliver you into our hands." And, of course, that's exactly what happened. David slew Goliath and went on to become the greatest king in the history of Israel.

As king, David would not always retain the wisdom he exhibited in his youth. He would forget what made him unique and slip into the kind of shady behavior so common among most other kings. More often, however, he would be true to himself and not try to put on armor that didn't fit him. Most importantly, David never lost his greatest strength: his firmly held belief that what made him strong was faith in the Lord who saved.

{ *Where does your strength lie? Is there sometimes a temptation to put on what others think you should wear, instead of putting on what fits you best?*

day twelve
BABBLE ON

So Naaman went down and plunged in the Jordan seven times, according to the word of the man of God. His flesh became again like the flesh of a little child, and he was clean.
—2 Kings 5:14

I am good for about ten minutes of prayer time a day. When I wake in the morning, I try to be thankful for the gift of another day, and I ask God, "Why do I get two?" In the evening, I look back on the day to see if I lived a good answer to the question. Both of those times of day—the beginning and the end—are God-times for me.

It is during the rest of the day—meaning most of the day—that I don't do so well. I lack mindfulness. When I try to pray during the day, I mostly just babble inside my head as random thoughts bubble up. My mind drifts to everything but God, caught up in wondering about things like why I received so many scented bath soaps for my birthday, or what that guy meant when he asked me if I'm surprised that I've been able to keep my job for so long.

I have made some strides of late by following advice from Jesus: "In praying, do not babble like the pagans. . . . Your father knows what you need before you ask him" (Matt. 6:7–9). The anti-babble measure I've taken is setting my watch to go off every day at 1:01. When it buzzes, I ask God, "What do I need?" I focus on that question because it is so specific—it keeps me from drifting—and because the thought that God knows the answer before I ask the question comforts me.

Which brings me to the story of Naaman, the great commander of the armies of Aram, a kingdom near Israel.

Namaan had leprosy. When he heard that healing might be had in Israel, he traveled there and sought out the Prophet Elisha. A valiant warrior, Namaan assumed that Elisha would give him some heroic task to accomplish to earn a cure. Elisha instead told Namaan to go and bathe in the Jordan River seven times. This angered Namaan. It was too simple, mundane. Also, there were plenty of better rivers in his homeland; the Jordan was so ordinary. But Namaan did as Elisha commanded him to do and was cured.

When I ask God what I need at 1:01 every day, the answer I usually hear is that, like Naaman, I need healing of some kind. It's generally for small cuts—an email that angered me, anxiety about one of our children, frustration with someone who refused to see things the right way (meaning my way). Sometimes, though, it's leprosy stuff—deaths, severed relationships, devastating setbacks. The cure, regardless of the severity of the affliction, is best found in the ordinary river nearby.

For those small cuts, for example, the ordinary river is mindfulness. It's amazing how easily the healing comes when I just acknowledge to myself what I'm angered, anxious, or frustrated about . . . and then nothing more. Awareness—and the perspective that comes with it—is enough to bring relief. More is required for more serious afflictions, a deeper plunge and bathing longer. Seven times did Naaman bathe in the Jordan, "seven" being a perfect number in Scripture. But it is still an ordinary river that heals.

I remember when I traveled to my parents' home to be with my dad toward the end of his long illness. I sat in his bedroom for hours at a time, mostly in silence with only the sounds of the TV. It wasn't just my father who was in such poor health. For many years our relationship had been suffering from an absence of simple things like conversation and sharing. When I was getting ready to leave the last day—and we both knew it was our final time together—I took the plunge: "Dad, do you have any advice for how I should live my life?"

I waited for an answer . . . and waited. Finally, he wheezed out, "Well, son, just keep doing what you're doing, I guess." Those perfectly ordinary words have been balm for me over the years. A simple blessing. Our Father knows what we need before we ask for it.

{ *Take a 1:01 moment. God, what do I need? If it is healing, where is there an ordinary river nearby to bathe in?*

day thirteen
SIN OF PARTIALITY

That same night I washed and went into the courtyard.
Because of the heat I left my face uncovered. I did not know
there that sparrows were perched on the wall above me; their
warm droppings settled in my eyes, causing white scales
on them. **—Tobit 2:9–10**

The books in the Bible were written within a belief system that held that bad things happened to people because they were bad and good things happened to people because they were good. Take Tobit as an example: Pre-bird droppings, Tobit had been viewed as an upright man because he prospered. Public opinion changed when he was blinded. Tobit's wife said aloud what everyone must have been thinking: "Where are your charitable deeds now? Where are your righteous acts? Look! All that has happened to you is well known!" (Tobit 2:14). Blindness—and being ridiculed for how he was blinded—wasn't enough. Tobit also had to suffer the indignity of demotion from saint to sinner in the eyes of the world.

Fast forward a couple hundred years to another blind man. The disciples saw him and asked Jesus, "Rabbi, who sinned, this man or his parents, that he was born blind?" Jesus told them that neither the man nor his parents had sinned, and then cured the blind man. Constant questioning followed the healing, especially by the Pharisees, and things got heated. Finally, the formerly blind man rebuked the Pharisees when they tried to paint Jesus as a sinner: "If this man were not from God, he would not be able to do anything." The Pharisees put the cured man in his place: "You were born totally in sin, and are you trying to teach us?" (John 9:33–34).

That's exactly what the theology of reducing the unfortunate to sinner status and elevating the fortunate to favored status was designed to do. Put people in their place—and keep them there. It was easier to justify relegating the poor, blind, and lame to the fringe when society believed that they deserved to be there due to their sinfulness. Similarly, how satisfying it must have been for the wealthy and healthy to believe that their good fortune was their just desserts.

Jesus constantly attacked this warped theology by touching the untouchables and casting villains as the heroes of his stories. As such, Jesus was a (very) early adopter of the Equal Protection Clause—he truly believed that everyone should be treated equally without regard to their status. And Jesus rejected outright the absurd belief that sinners were only getting what they deserved, and that the rich were rich because God favored them. Jesus was not, therefore, an early adopter of the Prosperity Gospel, that con being hawked by some preachers today that links faith in Jesus to wealth and health. There is nothing of the Gospels in that twisted gospel.

The early Christian community was very aware of the true gospel, and were especially mindful of how the poor should be treated: "For if a man with gold rings on his fingers and in fine clothes comes into your assembly, and a poor person in shabby clothes also comes in, and you pay attention to the one wearing the fine clothes and say, 'Sit here, please,' while you say to the poor one, 'Stand there,' or 'Sit at my feet,' have you not made distinctions among yourselves and become judges with evil designs?" (Jas. 2:2–4)

Scholars debate authorship of the Letter of James, but what is generally accepted is that it is not a letter. Rather, it's more like the wisdom literature found in Hebrew Scripture, with an emphasis on ethical conduct. Here the author condemned the "sin of partiality." Favoring those who had more over those who had less was completely contrary to early Christian belief and practice. Early Christians practiced instead the "royal law," called such because it came from God, the universal king: "However, if you fulfill the royal law according to the scripture, 'You shall love your neighbor as yourself,' you are doing well. But if you show partiality, you commit sin . . . " (Jas. 2:8–9).

It is good to just sit with the simple wisdom of the royal law. We do well when we treat people equally. We don't do well when we don't.

> *We could apply the sin of partiality to many of our interactions. For example, do I treat those who can do something for me differently from those who cannot?*

day fourteen
THE WORST
SCRIPTURE PASSAGE EVER

*Desolate Daughter Babylon, you shall be destroyed, blessed
the one who pays you back what you have done us! Blessed
the one who seizes your children and smashes them
against the rock.* **—Psalm 137:8–9**

Now that's a passage that sure sounds like a good argument
for atheism. How can it be, one might rightfully wonder, that
any faith could hold up as sacred Scripture the desire to smash
children against rocks? More fundamentally, how could anyone
believe in a god who would inspire followers to desire such things?

Attempts by experts to explain this passage away don't do
much to answer those questions. I recall, for example, watching
two religious pundits trying to wiggle their way out of this passage
by asking their television audience to substitute for "children" any
evil that plagues us. "Just pretend that what needs to be smashed
against rocks is the curse of drugs! See how this passage makes
sense now?"

Actually, no. This passage can't be explained away by
pretending it doesn't mean what the psalmist intended it to mean.
There are two steps to understanding Scripture: First, what was
the intended meaning of the passage? Second, what does it mean

to me? You can't just skip over the first step and go right to the second because a passage is difficult.

To figure out a possible intended meaning for this passage, it's best to start with context. (It's always best to start with context!) Babylonia conquered Judah in 587 BC, and the leadership of Jerusalem was forcibly removed to Babylon. What followed was the Babylonian Exile, a fifty-year captivity marked by humiliation, desperation, and the real fear that the faith would be blotted from history. The psalmist opened the hymn (psalms were meant to be sung) with the forlorn, "By the rivers of Babylon there we sat weeping when we remembered Zion [Jerusalem]." Eventually sadness morphed into rage as the psalmist recalled all that the Babylonians had done to his people and how difficult existence had become because of them. He exploded with the "seize your children and smash them against the rock" prayer. Please, God, destroy Babylon by destroying its future.

Scripture is God's Word in human terms. Everything that is written in the Bible has both God and human infused within it. That human infusion includes writing styles, historical context, and, yes, even emotional state. God's voice is usually clear, except when we run across a passage like this one. Still, there is at least a nugget of God's presence here, even if it can only be found in the negative.

The religious leaders who gathered some 2,000 years ago to decide what should be included in the sacred canon (Bible) must have paused, and even debated, when they got to this one. (Apparently the process involved a lot of debate. The Song of Songs, for example, was almost excluded because it was so sexually saucy that folks were singing it in bars.) I suspect that those religious leaders eventually decided to keep the smash-children psalm because it contains a key insight into who we are and how we relate to each other and God.

We are assured in the Genesis creation stories that we are made in God's image. We are also told in the sin stories that follow (Adam and Eve, Cain and Abel, etc.) that it's difficult for us to live fully in that image. We can only grow in our relationship with God and into the kind of people God wants us to be if we recognize just how inhumane we humans can be. While capable of so much good, we are also people who could pray that our enemy's children be smashed against rocks . . . or enslave races . . . or bring the Holocaust upon the earth. That's the "banality of evil" that was witnessed during the Nuremburg Trials after World War II. It wasn't that the Nazis looked like monsters that was so frightening; it's that they looked like everyone else.

God is speaking to us in this passage: Know thyself. Knowing that we can desire such horrible things doesn't bring much comfort, but it should make us more mindful. In that mindfulness, there is hope. That's why this psalm rightfully belongs in the Bible. Yes, we can become so angry that we could even pray for children to be smashed against rocks. That recognition should drive us to pray even harder that we never do. Pretending that we aren't capable of such hatred keeps that hatred closer at reach.

While it may be difficult to admit, is there a truly ugly hatred that sometimes wells up within you? How can this be brought to prayer?

day fifteen
BROKEN BUMPERS

The honesty of the upright guides them. **—Proverbs 11:3**

Someone once hit the rear of my parked car. Fortunately, he left a note. Then, a couple weeks later, the front of my parked car was hit. I was fortunate again; she too left a note.

I brought my car in for the repairs that the note-leavers agreed to pay for. When I picked it up, I mentioned to the service manager how lucky I was that both people left notes and how rare that must be. "Actually not," he said. "We've been seeing a lot of note-leaving lately."

That's the kind of feel-good story that I just can't keep to myself. So, I shared it on all-school prayer one morning. Good feelings, however, did not follow. Over the ensuing days I was sought out by students and teachers who told me about how different their experiences had been: "Hey, my parked car got hit once. No note." Every time there was a "humanity-sucks" edge to the comment. My response—"karma"—didn't seem to help.

I even heard stories about note-fakers. Someone hits a parked car and then, fearful that the accident was observed by a bystander, leaves a note on the windshield that is either blank or includes a hastily scrawled, "Good luck," with a smiley face affixed at the end.

This got me to wondering: Could the world be separated into three kinds of people? There are those who hit parked cars and leave real notes; those who hit parked cars and leave fake notes; and those who hit parked cars and just leave.

Of those last two not-so-good types, I prefer those who hit cars and just leave. At least they come by their dishonesty honestly. That type is following animal instincts embedded in our DNA—the fight or flight response (mostly flight). There's no malice aforethought. There's not much thought at all. Survival of the fastest (in getting away).

Note-fakers are worse because they are plotters who manipulate their surroundings to suit their selfish ends. Dishonesty compounded by the additional dishonesty of trying to appear honest, a phenomenon that's been popularized as "truthiness." From there it gets worse. As the lines between honesty and dishonesty are blurred, our desire and ability to separate the two diminishes. That is where we really start sliding down the slope, perhaps to that dangerous place where, as was once pronounced by a nationally known politician, "truth isn't truth." From there we bottom out in an Orwellian dystopia where 2+2=5.

A little over the top? Probably. But those two not-so-good types are real threats. If our culture is dominated by those who hit parked cars and flee then we've been reduced to the animal kingdom. If note-fakers ascend, then our culture, which depends upon most of us valuing truth and doing the honest thing, crashes to the ground.

Peter Maurin, co-founder of the Catholic Worker movement, said, "We must make the kind of society in which it is easier for people to be good." A good society requires that most of us lead honest, note-leaver lives. How do we get more of them and less of the other two?

Plato would say that note-leavers are born, not made. However, at the risk of getting invited to one of the "drunk philosophy" nights that have become so popular in Seattle bars, I propose that Aristotle's take was the right one: "We do not act rightly because we have virtue or excellence, but we rather have those because we have acted rightly. We are what we repeatedly do."

That's just common sense, and, when we are at our best, that is the philosophy that permeates our culture. A healthy, truth-centered society only gets that way if most individuals in that society consistently practice honesty and truthfulness in little ways. "We are what we repeatedly do." It's a life choice that is dependent upon daily choices.

If we are indeed now living in a time when note-faker and hit-and-flee types are proliferating, would that be the harbinger of a virtue apocalypse? Yes. But I've got a golden ticket that says different. Two of them in fact, both left on the windshield of my car.

{ *Which of the three is the most accurate description for you: Note-leaver, Fake-note-leaver, or Just-a-leaver?*

day sixteen
WHY DO I GET TWO?

*There is an appointed time for everything, and a time for
every affair under the heavens.* —**Ecclesiastes 3:1**

Every morning I say a prayer to myself that I've adapted from
a G. K. Chesterton poem: "Yesterday ended another day in
which I had eyes, ears, hands and the great world around me.
Today begins another day. Why do I get two?" I then ask myself
the same question at the end of the day, hoping that I will find a
good answer.

One day every one of us will stop getting two. That's not a
morbid thought. Rather, being mindful that our time on earth is
finite can and should lead to living purposefully. A new day isn't
just another day. It's an opportunity. There is a reason each of us
is alive; our time has a purpose under heaven. Each day gives us
a chance to live that purpose.

But this recognition can also be paralyzing. What is MY
PURPOSE? What is THE MEANING of my life? Those are
important questions, and we should pray over them, asking God
for guidance and wisdom. The problem is that we may never find
THE ANSWER to those questions. And if we spend our lives
trying to find THE ANSWER, we will likely miss the answers that
manifest themselves in daily living.

It is better to live a life of purposes than to obsess over the purposeful life. Why do I get two? Because, throughout the day, my eyes will see, and my ears will hear opportunities in this great world around me. Hopefully, my hands will seize those opportunities. As I look back at the end of the day, I can see purposes in those opportunities. String a lot of those days together and those purposes just might lead to PURPOSE, that place where God is calling me "to live and move and have my being."

One morning as I walked onto our school campus, I concluded my prayer with the customary question, "Why do I get two?" Just as I said those words to myself, I looked down and saw this big bag of dog poop. I don't like touching dog poop, even if it's surrounded by plastic. But I (reluctantly) picked it up and disposed of it anyway, just as I try to pick up any garbage I see as I walk around campus. That's a habit I got into long ago. Since I am a head of school, that physical act repeated often reminds me that I am a caretaker. Taking care of smaller things is interwoven with taking care of bigger things. Also, not picking up garbage would mean that I think that someone else should pick it up, a habit that would make me even more self-centered than I already am.

I do recognize that focusing on small things could result in small-mindedness. I remember seeing these words on a school reader board: "Go to Class. Be Nice." I asked our young son who was in the car with me what he thought of it, to which he replied, "Isn't that kind of like saying, 'blah, blah, blah?'" Wise lad. Being mindful of small things, however, need not reduce us to small thinking. There's a place for holy boldness in our lives, stretching ourselves toward BIG, PURPOSEFUL MEANING.

Generally, however, the best way to get to those grandiose times is through small moments that point us in that direction.

Greek philosophers spoke of teleology, the connection between a starting point and an ending point. The search for purposeful living started on one end can be successfully concluded with the discovery of purposeful living on the other end only by the dots lived in between those two points.

A few years ago, I met with a college graduate who wanted to talk about his career plans. With much excitement he described how he wanted to go to Central America so that he could teach coffee growers about sustainable farming practices. Lot of meaning in that big purpose! I asked him, "How much do you know about that kind of farming?" "I've read some good articles," he said. "Ok, can you speak Spanish?" He confided that his Spanish wasn't very bueno. I ended up suggesting that his first step down this path might be to work as a barista. "Start from the grounds up."

This young man sincerely desired to take that giant leap from where he was to where he wanted to be. I admired his vision. But it doesn't take a Greek philosopher to see that bridging the great expanse from the desire to live purposefully to living purposefully requires a lot of connections in between.

I end every day with this prayer: "Please, Lord, show me those times this day when I responded with love to your loving presence in my life, and those times when I did not." Immediately, purpose-opportunities come to mind, those I seized and those I didn't. I then conclude with what I believe to be the two most essential end-of-day prayers: "Thank you," and "Oh, well."

As you look over the dots of your life, do you see them connecting toward the place you want to go?

day seventeen
THE PERFECTION ILLUSION

*Better is one handful with tranquility than two with toil and
a chase after wind!* **—Ecclesiastes 4:6**

Something I've never seen in a college admissions brochure:
"We're better than some, not as good as most." Colleges—
especially the "elite" ones—instead hawk themselves as the only
place to be if you really want to be someone. All students live
perfectly balanced lives; every course is life-changing, every
experience exhilarating. There's the student pictured while
laboring in a lab on the cusp of a cure for cancer. Another is
shown scuba diving off the Barrier Reef. Finally, there's the shot
of the student curing cancer while scuba diving.

This hyped-up approach to college admissions turns young
heads away from looking for the right fit (the one handful with
tranquility) so that they can chase after the wind toward the
illusory promise of the perfect one. I suppose, however, that
chasing the wind when making college decisions does at least
prepare young people for what awaits in life. One handful is
never enough; we're supposed to toil for that something more
that, once gotten, must surely bring tranquility and fulfillment.

It's all part of the perfection illusion. Enough never feels good
enough because there's always that something better hovering on

the horizon: the perfect college, job, partner, children, friends, home. We see this a lot on social media—the pressure to post only beautiful faces in the most happening places. It's like the Carly Simon song "You're So Vain," with its lyric about being where we should be all the time. Even the Grand Canyon isn't picture-worthy enough. It's got to be the selfie at the edge of the Grand Canyon—which is why people have been falling to their deaths in record numbers there.

Living the perfection illusion is hamster wheel living. It leads nowhere. And it's also a missed opportunity. Because what is best in life is often found in pedestrian places, unscripted moments, and with the not-so-beautiful, even scarred, people who are never pictured in marketing materials.

When I was in law school most of my friends clerked at prestigious downtown firms. I didn't. I ended up where no one wanted to go—an obscure, blue-collar firm in a rough part of Milwaukee. But what I learned there about the law and life was something that just couldn't be taught while sitting in pristine, perfectly spaced cubicles doing research.

A lot of my work was in probate and bankruptcy. Death and debt. Widows and those who'd lost life savings due to medical expenses taught me how to be a more human lawyer. I also learned to admire small business owners, the effort and sacrifice required to keep afloat. My crowning achievement as a law clerk was the incorporation of Bunk Bed City and Mattress World, an accomplishment that let the good people of South Milwaukee sleep a little better at night.

The firm even had me serve legal papers on people we were suing, including a local candy shop owner. How hard can it be, I thought, to serve process on the Candyman, the guy who, as the song goes, can take a sunrise, sprinkle it with dew, cover it with chocolate and a miracle or two? That's when I learned that the Candyman keeps a baseball bat behind the counter and, even at 300 pounds, can jump over said counter with said baseball bat and chase me down the street. That experience taught me to question assumptions, and to get in better shape.

The firm was headed up by the not-so-beautiful, belligerent, cigar chain-smoking Steve Enich, a former NFL player for the Chicago Cardinals who was rumored to be a gun smuggler for Serbian rebels. When you gave Mr. Enich an answer he didn't like, he'd just punch you on the shoulder. Really hard.

One day Mr. Enich called me into his office. He showed me two circles he'd drawn: "These are two stadiums. The Packers are playing in one, and Jesus is in the other. Which one are you going to?" Not really thinking, I asked, "Who are the Packers playing?" This earned me a punch on the shoulder. "You don't know where to stand, Hickey, because you have no idea what you stand for." I needed to hear those words; I just never would have imagined that Steve Enich would be the one to say them to me.

There wasn't anything perfect about my experiences or the people at that law firm. How lucky I was. It turns out that filling up our lives with only the stuff used to fill in applications is chasing the wind. Often the best place is the one few want to go to. And sometimes the most thought-provoking people in our lives are the ones we'd not thought much of at all. Life is beautifully disheveled, more improvisation than script. That's handful enough.

It is said that the perfect is the enemy of the good. Where is there a movement within you to be more content with the good in life, even if it's not perfect?

day eighteen
A BAPTISM OF SORTS

*My son, from your youth choose discipline; and when you
have gray hair you will find wisdom.* —**Sirach 6:18**

One day, many years ago, I was a young teacher at an all-boys
Catholic high school in Milwaukee seated in a restroom
stall during a quiet study period trying to catch a few moments
of peace. I heard a sound and looked up, just as a bucket of water
was dumped on my head.

Quick and agile back then, I rushed out of the restroom and
caught the bucket-dumper in the hallway. Grabbing the miscreant
by the shirt, I shoved him up against the wall and screamed into
his face, "What the hell were you doing?" Then I sent him to the
Dean of Men, so that punishment could be exacted.

As time went on, I got a chance to know that freshman
(John) and am glad that I did; he was a terrific young person.
I recall giving him my favorite graduation gift four years later,
Merton's *The Seven Storey Mountain*. I lost touch with John after
he graduated and went off to Notre Dame.

Fast forward 30 years. John called me to let me know that
he was in Seattle for a conference and wanted to get together.
We went to breakfast and had a great visit. I was so happy to
hear about how well John was doing. A surgeon in Chicago, John

was blessed with a lovely wife and four beautiful children. At one point we laughed as we recalled the encounter that brought us together. I then asked John a question I had never asked him: "Why did you do it?"

John told me that the dumping moment was a pivotal one in his life. He had been trying to find a way to fit in with the cool kids and, when a couple of them urged him to do the water dump, he saw a way into the in-crowd. Part of the punishment exacted by the Dean of Men was a requirement that John reflect upon what he had done and why he had done it. That's when John recognized that his desire to be with the cool kids wasn't a healthy desire. He decided to go down a different path from that day forward.

John had found wisdom well before he found his hair turning gray. The discipline he began practicing was to not fall into the trap of sacrificing his values and identity for shiny, bright objects. That desire to belong to the in-crowd is a strong desire in one's freshman year of high school . . . and in a lot of years after that. Pushing that desire aside is hard work, a force of will that requires significant self-discipline.

And how about that young teacher who pushed a freshman up against the wall and screamed at him? Not a lot of self-discipline there. I thought a lot about it then, and it still pops into my head occasionally today. Why did I do that?

I think there were two reasons. One was my own desire to be in with the cool kids. As a young teacher in an all-boys school, I wanted to make sure that I was no one to mess with, just like the most admired older teachers at our school. The teachers' lounge in those days was a tough, chain-smoking, feral environment. I wanted to belong.

The other reason was my temper, a short fuse that mastered me. I was literally shaking when I held John up against that wall, and it wasn't because I was drenched in cold water. I wanted to hit this little freshman. Thankfully, though, a better angel saved me from my volatile nature.

Shortly after the incident I talked with a good Jesuit friend about my lack of self-discipline, especially how much anger owned me. "Pray over this," he said: "For what are you willing to crucify someone?" Nothing came to my mind then and, thankfully, as I've asked myself that same question over the years, there's still nothing that comes to mind.

Greater (though far from perfect) self-discipline has grown within me over the years as I've kept that Jesuit's question in mind. This now gray-haired teacher is the wiser for it.

{ *Where is greater self-discipline needed in your life and what practices would cultivate it?*

day nineteen
DEEP ROOTED

*Blessed are those who trust in the L*ORD*; the L*ORD *will be their trust. They are like a tree planted beside the waters that stretches out its roots to the stream: It does not fear heat when it comes, its leaves stay green; In the year of drought it shows no distress, but still produces fruit.*
—Jeremiah 17:7–8

I recall listening to a psychologist tell this story while explaining the interplay between anxiety and hope:

On Christmas Eve a couple placed very different gifts into the stockings of their young twins: a precious gold watch in one stocking, horse manure in the other. On Christmas morning, one twin slowly entered her parents' bedroom, nervously cradling the gold watch in her hands. "Mom and dad, this watch Santa left me is so pretty, but I'm afraid it will break. Can I hide it somewhere?" Then the other twin bounded into the bedroom, so excited she could barely contain herself: "You won't believe it! Santa brought me a pony—now I just need to find it!"

Wouldn't life be perfect if we could approach every experience with the boundless optimism of pony-manure-in-stocking girl? Not if we stop to think about it. That would mean living completely detached from critical thought. Not only did this kid think that

Santa delivered ponies, she also believed that Santa could train them to deposit manure into stockings.

The other twin represents the opposite extreme—the one where many of us often reside. Gold-watch-girl sees the world only as it is, especially all its dangers. She's also highly sensitive, which means she worries. A lot. This can be overwhelming, even debilitating. It's not that she cares too much, because there is no such thing. What's missing from her life is trust, and the hopefulness it brings.

Gold watch-girl reminds me of the Prophet Jeremiah, a young man with a sensitive soul who saw no gift in God's call. He was tasked with telling the people of Jerusalem what the Babylonians were going to do to them: "Four kinds of scourge I have decreed against them . . . the sword to kill them; dogs to drag them about; the birds of the sky and the beasts of the earth to devour and destroy them. And I will make them an object of horror to all the kingdoms . . . " (Jer. 15:3–4).

That was certainly cause for worry. And so was what followed: Jeremiah was reviled and mocked, placed in stocks at one time, thrown down a well another. Jeremiah was overwhelmed, bereft of hope: "You duped me, O LORD, and I let myself be duped . . . Cursed be the day on which I was born!" (Jer. 20:7,14 [NAB]). He also lost what little trust he had in God: "Why is my pain continuous, my wound incurable, refusing to be healed? To me you are like a deceptive brook, waters that cannot be relied on!" (Jer. 15:18).

There are a lot of prophets to choose from when teaching Scripture. I make sure that one of them is Jeremiah. It is likely that I have many more gold-watch-might-break students in class than I do pony-poop-in-stocking kids, and Jeremiah speaks to those anxious ones. It could also be because I am more of a worrier myself. I recall when I was a young father, for example, that I took a lesson from a parenting magazine and adopted a worry tree in our front yard. I was to place my hands on the tree every evening when I came home, depositing my worries there before entering the house. It didn't work. I kept forgetting to do it, mostly because I had too many worries on my mind.

When I talk with students about their worries, and I reflect upon my own, Jeremiah provides great comfort. Many of us worry—our lives often give us a lot to worry about. Jeremiah—the prophet of worry—became less worrisome and more hopeful when he decided to trust God. At those trusting times, Jeremiah too adopted a tree, one with roots in a stream—a tree that, in a year of drought, "shows no distress, but still produces fruit." With greater trust a little girl can receive a gold watch without being stressed out, and we can acknowledge our worries without being overwhelmed by them, living more in hope than anxiety. That is when we, like Jeremiah, can hear God with a more comforting voice: "For I know well the plans I have in mind for you . . . plans for your welfare and not for woe, so as to give you a future of hope" (Jer. 29:11).

Jesus talked a lot about the anxiety that comes when we feel like life is shoveling manure at us. What shall we make of these words: "Can any of you by worrying add a single moment to your life-span?" (Matt. 6:27)

day twenty
AN UNCARPETED WORLD

"[W]ith a sudden blow I am taking away from you
the delight of your eyes, but do not mourn or weep or
shed any tears. Groan, moan for the dead, but make no
public lament; bind on your turban, put your sandals
on your feet, but do not cover your beard or eat the
bread of mourners." In the evening my wife died. The
next morning I did as I had been commanded.
—Ezekiel 24:16–18

What is the greatest American novel? I would cast my vote for *All the King's Men* by Robert Penn Warren. It is so beautifully written, its exploration of power is timeless, and the characters are unforgettable. That includes Jack Burden, the novel's narrator, though he's frustrating to be with throughout much of the story. Jack is so reluctant to attach to anything or anyone; he just drifts. When he finally does attach, he does so by becoming involved in . . . tax policy. Certainly not exciting, let's-change-the-world kind of stuff. But Robert Penn Warren was brilliant for choosing tax policy as Jack's entry into making a difference; it's boring, unglamorous, requires hard work, and really matters to people and how they live their lives.

Ezekiel was doing something similar in this passage, although we can only know that by first understanding its historical context.

Prophets often shocked so that their message would be heard by people who didn't want to hear it. That's what Ezekiel was doing by not grieving when his wife died. That callousness certainly got a reaction. Ezekiel used it to drive home the message God had entrusted to him.

Ezekiel and other leaders had been exiled to Babylon. There, they awaited word of the fate of Jerusalem, the beloved city of God. That "wife" was about to die. But Ezekiel and other leaders were not to mourn when they learned of Jerusalem's destruction. They were to instead immediately get to work while in exile so that the faith would be kept alive. Everything depended upon their efforts.

That's the historical context. Then there's the context we all share, regardless of time or place: Being human means experiencing hardships. Sometimes it's the big stuff—the death of a loved one. More often it's the middling junk, death by 10,000 cuts. Either way, life's blows can be really disheartening, lamentable. Yet, there are times when we simply must groan in silence, bind up our turbans, put on our sandals, and do the work that must be done.

None of this means that we shouldn't grieve in loss, or seek some comfort when challenges become overwhelming. Our mental and emotional health depends upon seeking relief when we are stressed out. But the work remains, as does the hard, rough ground we sometimes walk on. As *Saturday Night Live*'s Stuart Smalley once said: "It's easier to put on slippers than to carpet the whole world." Only the Garden of Eden is carpeted;

everywhere else is covered in rough patches, and those are the places we walk on most.

Those exiles in Babylon provide an instructive and inspirational example for us. They did indeed go immediately to their work after Jerusalem fell and the temple was destroyed. The exiles compiled the various writings of their faith tradition (especially what we now know as the Pentateuch, or Torah); developed a way to practice their religion without a temple; and kept their faith alive when it could very well have died out. When the Babylonian Exile ended 50 years later what emerged was modern Judaism, a rebirth of the faith. None of that would have happened if Ezekiel and other Jewish leaders had wallowed in their hardships.

It's no secret that our world is experiencing numerous hardships today, many of our own making. But every generation encounters its bad stuff that it needs to work through. None of what we face today, for example, compares to what the generation that faced the Great Depression and the Nazi threat had to overcome. Each of us, in every generation, is called to do something, even if the contribution is a grain of sand shared for the common good. We could withhold what we should contribute, lamenting that the world is not carpeted at our feet, but no good would come from that. It's not a happy thought, though it's a true one: Life's work is not cushy work.

{ *One way to not feel overwhelmed by the problems of the world is to work on one of those problems. What would be a good one to work on?*

day twenty-one
THE PUNY PROPHET

Jonah was greatly delighted with the plant.

—Jonah 4:6

The Book of Jonah was written in the fifth century BC, shortly after the Jewish people had been allowed to return to Israel after their 50-year forced exile in Babylon. They were a changed people. In one sense the change was positive, as seen in a renewed commitment to the faith and increased devotion to religious practices. In another sense, it was not.

The pain and humiliation of the Babylonian Captivity had scarred these people, causing many to turn inward. As they grew more reclusive, they also became more exclusive. Outsiders were viewed as threats, better kept at a distance. Many came to believe that God's mercy was reserved only to those of the Jewish faith.

The brilliant anonymous author of the Book of Jonah poked holes in this exclusivist post-exilic mindset through humor. The literary form is satire, better read as something like a Mark Twain story than the other prophetic books. Like all good satirists, the author of Jonah lampooned straight and true, and probably made enemies while doing so.

The first part of the story is well known. God called Jonah to prophesy to the Assyrians, the eighth-century enemy of Israel who served as the stand-in for all outsiders in the story. God wanted the Assyrians to repent from their sins and turn to goodness. Jonah, who most certainly did not like Assyrians, wanted no part in their salvation. So, Jonah sailed away from God, a trip that concluded with Jonah being spit up on the shore after having spent three days in the belly of a big fish.

Here, finally, Jonah relented and did what God had commanded him to do. Jonah traveled to Nineveh, the capital of Assyria, and walked around while shouting: "Forty days more and Nineveh shall be destroyed." It's here that we should remind ourselves that, almost always when prophets talked, no one listened. Not so for Jonah. His likely half-hearted calls to repentance had an immediate impact. Everyone in Nineveh repented, including the king, who took off his robes and sat in ashes while wearing sackcloth. There's even a biblical first: the animals also repented— they too took to wearing sackcloth.

All of this should have made Jonah very happy. With little effort or enthusiasm, his was the voice that led to the greatest mass repentance in biblical history. But Jonah wasn't happy at all. He bitterly called out God in one of the most non-condemning condemnations in the Bible: "I knew that you are a gracious and merciful God, slow to anger, abounding in kindness, repenting of punishment" (Jonah 4:2). The last god that Jonah wanted was this God, big-hearted enough to show mercy to outsiders who deserved no mercy. Jonah saw no reason to live if it meant being stuck with such a flawed deity: "Take my life from me. . . ."

But God didn't take Jonah's life. So, Jonah sulked away from Nineveh and made camp in a place that would give him a good view of the city's destruction should God decide to end all this nonsense by ending the Ninevites' existence. Jonah watched and stewed. Then he got heated; the sun was relentless. God soothed Jonah by causing a big gourd plant to grow and provide some shade.

Then, inexplicably, God sent forth a worm to attack the gourd plant and it died. Jonah was livid. Instead of killing the Ninevites, God killed off the plant that gave Jonah shade. It's pray-for-death time again. God asked Jonah why he was so angry. "I have reason to be angry," Jonah answered, "ANGRY ENOUGH TO DIE." (My capitalization to match Jonah's sense for the dramatic.)

Have you ever felt puny? Like rampage-over-a-missing-Twinkie-in-the-break-room puny? It's only afterward, with a little reflection, that the Twinkie's importance is brought to scale. That's the point of the gourd story. God called out Jonah on his puniness, and, in doing so, gave us one of the best perspective lessons in all of Scripture:

"You are concerned over the plant which cost you no labor and which you did not raise; it came up in one night and in one night it perished. And should I not be concerned over Nineveh, the great city, in which there are more than a hundred and twenty thousand persons who cannot distinguish their right hand from their left, not to mention the many cattle?" (NAB)

That's how the book ends. God's concern stretches far and wide, from those inside the faith to those outside, even cattle wearing sackcloth.

{ *Who are the outsiders today who could use more care?*

day twenty-two
BROTHER'S KEEPER

*[L]ove your enemies, and pray for those who persecute you,
that you may be children of your heavenly Father, for he
makes his sun rise on the bad and the good, and causes rain
to fall on the just and the unjust.* —**Matthew 5:44–45**

I believe it was Henri Nouwen who said that "community is that place where the person I least want to live with lives." It's easy to care for others—to live in community—in the abstract. It gets harder in real life when the "other" moves from people in general to the person you are sharing an office with who takes off his shoes and socks so that he can clip his toenails.

The French philosopher Jean-Paul Sartre believed that "hell is other people." For Sartre that was likely true, given that he spent his days in Parisian cafes wearing black and bemoaning the emptiness of existence and the absurdity of life. For the rest of us, hell isn't the population in general. It is a specific person in a specific situation who is hellish.

That is what makes Jesus's "love your enemies" teaching so spot on, and so difficult. We can't know if Jesus was thinking about a particular enemy in his own life when he said this, but I suspect that he was. Maybe, for example, Jesus was thinking about this one scribe who was especially abrasive, constantly asking questions designed to entrap Jesus. Or, perhaps it was Jesus's old neighbors in Nazareth, the ones who tried to throw him off a cliff when he went home to visit his mom.

I have often wondered if Jesus had someone from Scripture in mind when he called us to love even the bad, unjust people in our lives. That is when I think about Cain, likely the most despicable person in Hebrew Scripture. Cain was jealous, ungrateful, and the possessor of murderous rage. Add to that his propensity to be self-righteous and smug when he was called out for his bad behavior, and we are left with one hellish character.

Cain's sin is well-known: Cain became "resentful and crestfallen" when God favored Abel's offering over his own. So, Cain invited Abel out into the field and killed him. God arrived and asked Cain, "Where is your brother Abel?" With that came Cain's chance at redemption—an honest reckoning with God. Instead, Cain snapped back with, "I do not know. Am I my brother's keeper?" (Gen. 4:9).

It's a rhetorical question. Cain definitely did not see himself as his brother's keeper—we know that because he had just murdered him. Cain then went on to compound his extreme violence with extreme arrogance. In the "brother's keeper" question, Cain essentially told God to get lost. Literally caught red-handed, Cain remained an entitled, self-centered, mean-spirited young man. (Maybe that's why Cain's gift was rejected in the first place. The gift, like Cain, was covered in resentment.)

Cain didn't get any better as the story moved along. God spared Cain eye-for-eye justice, punishing him with banishment instead of execution. Was Cain grateful? Decidedly not. Cain complained to God that banishment would make him vulnerable to attack (more than a little ironic given what he'd just done to his brother). So, God showed even greater mercy to Cain, placing a mark on him that would protect Cain from harm. God kept caring for Cain, even when there was so little to care for.

God's care for Cain is why I think Jesus may have had Cain in mind when he said that we are to love our enemies. Cain remained a child of the heavenly Father, even after all that he'd done. We—all of us—remain children of the heavenly Father even after all we've done. We all carry some Cain within, including our inclination to murder in our hearts, but God keeps us anyway. Even when we are living throw-away lives and there isn't much to love about us, God continues to find us loveable.

Jesus wasn't telling us to love only loveable types; he was telling us to love Cain types. In doing so, Jesus confirmed the brother's keeper teaching while recognizing its difficulty: To love the bad and the good, the just and the unjust, in rain or no rain, at sunrise and sunset, always. God's way is a different way, and that includes loving those we would rather just keep away.

{ *Is it possible to truly love the Cains encountered in life, or is the "love your enemies" teaching mostly wishful thinking?*

day twenty-three
DISORDERED TREASURES

"For where your treasure is,
there also will your heart be."
—Matthew 6:21

have always enjoyed writing. It's a simple, honest pleasure for me.

That was my experience when I was writing my first book, *Finding Your Posts.* I know it's not deep, transformative literature. It includes my workout playlist (accompanied by very sweaty workout pictures) and "wisdom" I learned while in Vegas for my fiftieth birthday. But I really enjoyed writing that little book and felt a healthy pride when it was done.

I intended to just give out *Posts* to the audiences I had in mind when I wrote it: school parents and high school seniors. But then I decided to sell it on Amazon. That moved me a little away from the simplicity of the original goal, but not too far. Sales spiked immediately after the book was launched—my mom has a lot of friends. That felt good. But I wanted to feel better.

So, I researched how *Posts* might move up in Amazon rankings. I found out that the key is to switch from general categories to obscure ones. "Christian self-help" appeared promising, so I moved *Posts* there and watched it climb.

Mind you, in a narrow category like "Christian self-help" it only takes two sales to leap ten spots. Nevertheless, I was pumped. I began clicking on where *Posts* was ranked daily, and then five-six times a day. *Posts* surged into the Top 10, but that wasn't enough for me. I wanted to enter the Promised Land that only an Amazon Fulfillment Center could deliver: Best Seller in my category. I began checking hourly. *Posts* kept climbing. That best seller blue ribbon was within my grasp!

Then it happened. *Pregnant by a Bad Boy* came out of nowhere and surged ahead of *Posts*. WTFudge! *Bad Boy* had this chiseled, tattooed, bare-chested Fabio-type on the cover, clearly just a salacious read placed in an obscure category to increase rankings. What a fraud. My mom's friends, stretched thin on their fixed incomes due to *Posts* purchases, could no longer prop up my book in the rankings. *Posts* dropped out of the Top 100, and shortly thereafter sank into Amazon oblivion: the $.99 cart.

Pregnant by a Bad Boy was a great gift to me. I recognized that I was the one who was the fraud. The simple joy of writing and the healthy pride I had taken in my little book had devolved into something not very healthy at all. St. Ignatius called what I had slipped into a "disordered attachment." We lose ourselves when we treasure things that are alien to our true selves. Riches, pride, and, in the case for me with my *Posts* obsession, honors, can take hold of our hearts. And, since hands follow the heart, our actions flow from those unhealthy desires.

Disordered attachments can be anything. Look, for example, at a parent desiring that her child attend an excellent college as a springboard for a wonderful life. So much good can flow from that desire if it remains a healthy one. That's when we hear about a single mom working three jobs to help pay for her child to become the first in the family to go to college. Then we look at pictures of their faces on graduation day. So healthy, so pure, because it comes from a good spirit and stays there.

But what happens when that desire for a child to go to an excellent college comes more from the desire to be able to talk about it at cocktail parties? When the desire shifts from what is good for the child to what looks good for the parent, everything changes. That desire—borne from pride—can even devolve into cheating and bribery.

Something similar can happen with the desire for riches. Getting kids addicted to nicotine with fruity tasting nicotine products, or marketing opioids as harmless while knowing that they are incredibly destructive, are truly monstrous acts. We are lying to ourselves, however, if we think that evil of that kind can only be committed by monsters. The people who did that are like all people. It is the desire for riches that takes hold, twists, and bends hearts toward malevolence.

There was once a woman in New Zealand who dropped dead because she drank two gallons of Coke a day. I'm sure that her excess didn't start out that way. But once we start down a destructive path, it's hard to get off it. That is a life lesson we can never stop learning. Luckily, if we pay attention, there is no shortage of warning signs. Thank you, *Pregnant by a Bad Boy.*

Jesus was tempted by the devil in the desert with riches, honors, and pride. (Matt. 4:1–11) Which of those three is most tempting?

day twenty-four
VIOLENT FAITH

The kingdom of heaven suffers violence, and the violent are taking it by force. —**Matthew 11:12**

What does the Kingdom of Heaven look like? Why, it's that place where peace and harmony reign, of course. Think of how smoothly things would have gone for Jesus if he had described it that way, all butterflies and rainbows. His anesthetized followers would have just nodded assent, as they nodded off. Maybe Jesus wouldn't have gotten himself killed if he and the Kingdom had been a little more . . . neutral.

Jesus, however, wasn't very good at marketing. He didn't sell the Kingdom as a stroll through lilies in the field, and he made it clear that it's no bed of roses: "Do not think that I have come to bring peace upon the earth. I have come to bring not peace but the sword" (Matt. 10:34).

That sword was present from the very beginning. King Herod reacted to the news of the birth of the Christ-child by ordering that the infants of Bethlehem be put to the sword. Addicted to power, Herod simply did what the powerful do when threatened: eliminate the threat. Jesus—born in poverty, humility, and powerlessness—represented a new way of being king and a new kind of Kingdom, one completely foreign to the likes of Herod. Herod tried to kill off that new Kingdom by killing off its new King.

The Kingdom of the Christ doesn't fit into the kingdoms of Herod types, yet it is Herod types (the materialistic, arrogant, and power-mad) who often hold sway in the world. There will always be conflict between Christ the King and those other kings; the Kingdom of Heaven will always suffer violence. And there will always be a stark choice between belonging to Christ's Kingdom and those other kingdoms. Dual citizenship isn't an option.

What about the second part of the passage, "and the violent are taking it by force." Here Jesus shifted from external conflicts to what belonging to his Kingdom does to us on the inside.

"Violence" should be seen more as passion, as in those who desire the Kingdom being akin to violent attackers of a city who desperately desire to possess all its treasures (Collegeville Biblical Commentary). As such, it's like other Kingdom parables: Someone finds treasure in a field and sells all to buy it, or a merchant uses all he owns to purchase the pearl of great price (Matt. 13:44–47). If Jesus were around today, he might describe the Kingdom with the Texas Hold 'Em parable—the gambler goes all in with his chips to win the pot.

The second part of the passage—"and the violent are taking it by force"—is translated in some Bibles as "and the violent bear it away." Discipleship carries with it a heavier burden in this translation: Those who decide to take Christ's Kingdom must then take Christ away with them. But bearing Christ within can feel unbearable. Choosing Christ and the Kingdom carries with it a personal cost: it cuts; it does violence to our insides. There is a sword here too.

When Mary and Joseph brought the baby Jesus to the Temple for consecration, they encountered Simeon, a devout, elderly man who yearned for the coming of the Christ. He was of Herod's Kingdom, but wanted another. Simeon looked upon the Christ-child and saw what he had been looking for, even praying for death because his greatest desire had been realized: "Now, Master, you may let your servant go in peace . . . for my eyes have seen your salvation" (Lk. 2:29–30).

But even that grace-filled moment suffered violence. Simeon looked upon Mary and told her how her life would change because Jesus had entered into it: "Behold, this child is destined for the fall and rise of many in Israel, to be a sign that will be contradicted (and you yourself a sword will pierce) . . ." (Lk. 2:22–38). And that is exactly what happened to Mary, especially as she looked upon her son on the cross.

Jesus pierces, and it is only with a pierced heart that the Kingdom of the Christ can be entered. Once that Kingdom is entered, the Kingdom of Herod is left behind. Just as the true Kingdom cannot be contained within Herod's puny world, so also the true King, Jesus, cannot be contained within puny hearts. Our hearts must be ripped open so that Jesus can enter through the gap.

My favorite character in the *Narnia Chronicles* is Eustace Scrubb, a greedy, selfish, nasty boy who is magically transformed into a dragon, an ugly exterior that reflects his interior ugliness. But it is in the pain of life as a dragon—estranged from humanity—that Eustace slowly learns how to be human. Though he remains a dragon in appearance, the heart of Eustace becomes generous, selfless, and empathetic.

The problem for Eustace, as it is for all of us, is that our own efforts are not enough. (That's why self-help books can offer only so much help.) Eustace does what he can. He peels away some of the dragon skin on his own and has a little success. But the transformation requires more: Eustace asks for the help of Aslan, the great lion-king (and Christ figure), and help is given: "The first tear he (Aslan) made was so deep that I thought it had gone right into my heart. And when he began pulling skin off, it hurt worse than anything I've ever felt."[4]

That's what Jesus seeping under the skin does to a body.

{ *What to make of this quotation from Flannery O'Connor: "All human nature vigorously resists grace because grace changes us and the change is painful."*

day twenty-five
PIGEON WISDOM

So (Jesus) was not able to perform any mighty deeds there, apart from curing a few sick people by laying his hands on them. He was amazed at their lack of faith. —**Mark 6:5–6**

Jesus was visiting his hometown, Nazareth. He probably was hoping for a warm reception, but that's not what he got. Instead, the townspeople treated Jesus with suspicion, disdain; they had no faith in him. This really affected Jesus, so much so that—and these are important words—Jesus was "not able" to perform any mighty deeds there.

Not that Jesus didn't want to perform miracles, or that there weren't any miracles to perform, but that Jesus was *unable* to perform them. In other words, Jesus needed people, especially their faith in him, to help people with mighty deeds.

We don't usually think of Jesus needing anything from us. God, after all, is all-powerful. But God loved us so much that God lived fully as a human: Jesus. And being human meant needing other humans, which is core to who we are. In living that, Jesus was teaching us how essential it is that we rely upon one another, especially in times of need.

This reminds me of a time I was sitting on my back porch when a pigeon landed next to my feet and just stayed there,

79

staring at me. This made me feel uncomfortable, so I got up and moved to another chair. The pigeon followed me and stared at me some more.

I didn't have any food, so that couldn't have been the reason why it followed me. Then I thought, maybe it was drawn to me because I am so pigeon-toed myself and it mistook me for kin. I looked into the pigeon's eyes. They were WILD eyes. They started moving side to side and up and down. I got anxious and began wondering, "Is there such a thing as pigeon rabies?" Sure, no teeth, but that beak looked like it could draw blood.

I moved again—this time quickly and to the other end of the porch. Once again, the pigeon followed me. Desperate for relief, I cried out to my wife, "There's a pigeon out here that won't leave me alone!"

When my wife came outside, she noticed a marking that indicated it was a racing pigeon. A little more sleuthing and an hour later a kind of pigeon-whisperer came to our house to pick up the pigeon. She explained that pigeons seek out humans when they get lost and disoriented. That is, when pigeons need help, they rely upon humans to give it to them.

At our best, we are all racing pigeons: fast, goal-driven, iron-willed, built for distance. Except when we are not. We sometimes fall to the ground—disoriented, lost, and looking for help.

When we are thriving and flying high, we need to look out for those who have been grounded. We can see it in their eyes, lost and disoriented. Even in our busy-ness—especially in our busy-ness—we should stop and come to their aid. And, when we ourselves are grounded, we must trust that others will do the same. Needing and relying upon each other: that's what being human is all about.

St. Paul wrote that "the Spirit comes to the aid of our weakness."
When we look up for the Holy Spirit—the dove descending from
above—it's a symbol of our belief that God's Spirit really is active
in the world. While that is reassuring, up above is not where the
Holy Spirit is most active. It is on the ground, especially in times
of need, when one of us is looking around with wild eyes in the
hopes that another of us will take notice and take action. In this
Spirit, we can do mighty deeds together.

{ *Know of anyone who has the wild eyes of the lost and
disoriented? What can be done?*

day twenty-six
MISFITTED

He replied . . . "But if you can do anything, have compassion on us and help us." Jesus said to him, "'If you can!' Everything is possible to one who has faith." Then the boy's father cried out, "I do believe, help my unbelief!" **—Mark 9:21–24**

No American novelist has helped our unbelief more than Flannery O'Connor, and few have been more misunderstood. O'Connor wrote darkly humorous stories set deep in the mid-twentieth-century South that revolved around unlikeable, even grotesque characters. Her stories were all about faith, without appearing to be about faith.

"Truth doesn't change according to our ability to stomach it," O'Connor said.[5] And much of what O'Connor wrote is certainly hard to stomach, so bizarre and violent. Writing during what is often referred to as the post-Christian era, O'Connor believed that, "You have to push as hard as the age that pushes against you." She wrote disturbing stories because she felt she had to, given her audience: ". . . to the hard of hearing you shout and for the almost blind you draw large and startling figures."[6]

O'Connor's most famous and most violent story is *A Good Man is Hard to Find.* The story revolves around a very foolish, self-absorbed grandmother, the matriarch of a very foolish, self-absorbed family. A wrong turn leads to a car accident, and the family is stranded in a remote part of the Georgia countryside. That's where The Misfit, a serial killer, comes upon them.

The story is about belief, the grandmother far removed from it and the Misfit who is right at its edge. The Misfit doesn't fit neatly into the world, and he knows it: "My daddy said I was a different breed of dog from my brothers and sisters. 'You know,' Daddy said, 'it's some that can live their whole life out without asking about it and it's others has to know why it is, and this boy is one of the latters. He's going to be into everything!" That needing-to-know-why-life-is draws The Misfit to Jesus for answers. The Misfit thinks about Jesus, lamenting that "He thrown everything off balance" when he rose from the dead. He is tormented by the thought of Jesus, hits the ground when he talks about Jesus, wishes he had been there to know Jesus.

The Misfit knows he has a choice, "to follow Him (Jesus) or enjoy yourself by doing some meanness to somebody. . . ."[7] He's poised and prepped for grace. But it doesn't happen. Or, more accurately, The Misfit doesn't take it when it's offered.

Grace is, instead, taken by the least likely character, the annoying, manipulative grandmother. There is nothing spiritual, thoughtful, or redeeming about the woman. There is no evidence that she had given any thought to Jesus; never was she tormented by his presence in the world. Yet, it's the grandmother who has the "I do believe" moment.

When I first read *Good Man*, I couldn't bring myself to accept that moment as a sincere one. I saw it as just a continuation of the grandmother's self-centeredness and manipulation. O'Connor set me straight: "All of my stories are about the action of grace on a character who is not very willing to support it . . .," and she cited the grandmother as a prime example. O'Connor takes Jesus at his word. Grace isn't earned; it's simply offered.

But few of us accept it. O'Connor said, "There is a moment of grace in most stories, or a moment when it is offered, and is usually rejected."[8] The Misfit is the Patron Saint of Rejected Grace, and we get a hint as to why in his conversation with the grandmother: " 'If you would pray,' the old lady said, 'Jesus would help you.' 'That's right,' The Misfit said. 'Well, then, why don't you pray?' she asked trembling with delight suddenly. 'I don't want no hep,' he said. 'I'm doing all right by myself.' "[9]

None of us are doing all right by ourselves, and we're fooling ourselves if we think differently. The Misfit—all of us—need the kind of "hep" that only comes to us on bended knee. "Help my unbelief!" The Misfit just couldn't bring himself to bend that knee and say those words. Still, there's hope for him. "I can fancy a character like the Misfit being redeemable," wrote O'Connor.[10] Fortunately for The Misfit, and for all of us, the harder the heart, the harder God works.

> *The Misfit valued his self-sufficiency so much that he couldn't bring himself to ask for God's help, even in his torment. God wants to help. Why not ask for it?*

day twenty-seven
SECOND CHANCES

At that statement his face fell, and he went away sad, for he had many possessions. —**Mark 10:22**

There lived long ago a young man who followed all the rules. He didn't steal, was respectful to his parents, and kept his word when he made promises. But he thought that goodness required more of him, so he sought out Jesus for advice.

The young man knelt before Jesus and asked him, "Good teacher, what must I do to inherit eternal life?" But what he was really asking was, "What do I need to do to be truly good?" Jesus looked into his heart and loved him; there was something to this young man. But Jesus also saw a problem in that heart: the young man was too attached to his possessions. What he owned had started to own him. So, Jesus gave the young man the advice that would set him free: "Go, sell what you have, and give to [the] poor and . . . follow me." At this the young man's "face fell" and he turned and went away sad. Jesus had asked much of him—too much—or so the young man thought.

Jesus went on to say right after the young man left that it is harder to pass through the eye of a needle than for a rich person to enter the Kingdom of Heaven. So, this is known as The Story of the Rich Young Man. It is that, but it is also more than that.

A few years ago, I was at a Mass celebrated by a Cardinal who gave a homily about the Story of the Rich Young Man. I recall hearing the Cardinal say that by rejecting Jesus's challenge the young man had forever cast his lot with "riches, power, and sex." How he was able to weave sex into the story I have no idea, but it was what the Cardinal said next that really bothered me: "With that one decision, the young man was forever exiled from the presence of Jesus, forever separated from goodness."

"Well, you're just dead wrong," I said inside my head. And then I looked around the Church to make sure I hadn't accidentally said this out loud, since sometimes my inner filter doesn't work so well.

Each and every one of us is made in God's image, imbued with God's goodness. And every day we are faced with the choice of living in that goodness . . . or not. No one outside the grave is "forever exiled" from the presence of God. No one decision forever condemns anyone to a life of evil, though it's also true that no one decision guarantees a lifetime of goodness. No decision is conclusive, although every decision is essential because every day we make ourselves more of what we are becoming.

Here's the story of another young man, one I heard from a wonderful diocesan priest many years ago: A senior got up to speak to his classmates on their final retreat together. He told them that he was happy to be with them because he nearly wasn't. Freshman year had been incredibly hard for him, at home and at school. He felt so hopeless and overwhelmed by the sadness and pressures of his life that, at the end of one school day, he cleaned out his locker, stuffed the contents in his bag, and walked out the front door of the school. He had vowed to himself that he would never return, loathing life so much that he was thinking about ending it.

On the way out the door he dropped his bag, and everything spilled to the ground. Most walked by, a couple laughed. But one girl, an upperclassman, didn't. She bent down and helped him pick up his stuff. Then she walked with him down the street to his bus stop, talking along the way. As she left him, she turned and asked, "See you tomorrow?" No answer. She wouldn't take no answer for an answer, so she asked again, "I'm going to see you tomorrow, yes?" "Yes," the freshman said. And he did.

That freshman, grown to a senior four years later, told his classmates that what that girl did for him that day saved him. But she likely never knew that. She just chose to do something good that day, likely part of a pattern of doing good that would bring her closer to eternal life. And, thankfully, that boy made a different decision as well the next day, and every day thereafter. Maybe he'll be joining her in the Kingdom.

And what of the rich young man? He wasn't up to the challenge Jesus had set forth before him on that one day. But what about the next day? Just maybe, that next day the young man showed up and had breakfast with Jesus, no longer wealthy, but freer to embrace the goodness that Jesus had seen within him.

Imagine asking, "What do I need to do to have eternal life?" while sitting at breakfast with Jesus. What does Jesus say in response?

day twenty-eight

MARY'S DECISION

And coming to her, (the angel) said, "Hail, favored one!
The Lord is with you." But she was greatly troubled at what
was said and pondered what sort of greeting this might be.
—Luke 1:28–29

When I was a little kid, I was afraid of being visited by ghosts. I even saw my own mother as a potential threat down the line. This bothered me so much that one day I asked her, "You won't haunt me when you die, right?" "Well, we'll see," she said.

I made a similar request of Mary and Jesus during prayer time at night. I wanted to grow closer to them, but not if that meant they would get too close to me. So, I often began my nightly prayer by asking Mary and Jesus to not appear in my bedroom. I was just too afraid.

Luke's Gospel tells of a ghostly visitor to Mary's bedroom, a story re-told every Advent. Whenever I listen to the reading I wonder if Mary was afraid. Luke describes Mary as having been "greatly troubled" by the appearance of the angel, words that probably do not capture how terrified Mary must have been.

The angel's greeting only added confusion to the fear: "Hail, favored one! The Lord is with you." Mary, in her troubled state, had to figure out what this greeting meant. Why was she being hailed as favored? How was the Lord with her? Luke writes that Mary "pondered." That quick transition from being terrified to pondering says a lot about Mary.

I picture Mary, who was likely a teenager when all this happened, as the different girl in the village. Not a bizarre different, but a bit of an oddity in how poised and reflective she was compared to her peers. Rather than blather and spout, Mary chewed on things, took them inside and reflected upon them. Mary lived a vibrant interior life, which likely didn't make her the life of the party. But hers was a calming, gentle presence that quietly comforted those around her.

The second part of the encounter with the angel also says a lot about Mary. Luke's description here mirrors a previous description, the visit of the angel to Zechariah. Gabriel is the visitor in both stories, and in both he tries to comfort ("Do not be afraid"). He also shares startling news in each account: Zechariah is told that his wife, Elizabeth, will bear a son (John) in her old age. Mary is told that she "will conceive in your womb and bear a son, and you shall name him Jesus."

What is different, however, is the reaction. Zechariah wanted more proof: "How shall I know this?" He is struck speechless by Gabriel, "because you did not believe my words, which will be fulfilled at their proper time." Mary also asked a question, "How can this be, since I have no relations with a man?" But the question didn't hint at disbelief. Rather, that pondering mind sincerely wanted to know how someone who'd not had sex could have a child.

It is hard to see how Gabriel's response could not have greatly troubled Mary again: The "Most High will overshadow you" and "the child to be born will be called holy, the Son of God." But in Mary's calm, poised response we see what made her most holy herself—trust in God, and God's will. "May it be done to me according to your word." Mary's faith in God dissolved her fear into acceptance; Mary's desire for God was absorbed into God's desire for her.

I no longer ask Mary and Jesus to stay out of my bedroom when I pray at night. Nor, however, do I ask them to come in. Maybe I am still afraid. Mary-faith is scary. She knew that accepting the angel's invitation would overturn her life, perhaps even expose her to the harshest extreme of the law. (The penalty for adultery by a betrothed maiden was death by stoning—Deuteronomy 22:23–24.) Yet, even knowing this, Mary said "yes;" no additional clarifying questions, no pre-conditions.

If Mary were to visit me, she might ask a terrifying question: "Are you willing to truly love my Son, even though it would upend your world and you?" That is probably why I'm greatly troubled at the thought of letting her near me.

{ *Using the gift of imagination, have a conversation with Mary. Does Mary ask a question?*

day twenty-nine

GOOD CONFESSIONS

Getting into one of the boats, the one belonging to Simon,
(Jesus) asked him to put out a short distance from the shore.
Then he sat down and taught the crowds from the boat. After
he had finished speaking, he said to Simon, "Put out into
deep water and lower your nets for a catch."... They came
and filled both boats so that they were in danger of sinking.
When Simon Peter saw this, he fell at the knees of Jesus and
said, "Depart from me, Lord, for I am a sinful man."
—Luke 5:3–8

Though the Gospel accounts vary, this story may describe Simon Peter's first encounter with Jesus. It began with Jesus getting into Simon Peter's boat and preaching to the crowd. Jesus's words must have deeply affected Simon Peter because, though he had just met him, Simon Peter called Jesus "Master." Simon Peter also immediately trusted Jesus. He did not hesitate to put his boats back out when Jesus requested it, even though Simon Peter believed there were no fish to catch. Miraculously, so many fish were caught that both boats nearly sank.

Simon Peter encountered the full force of Jesus—a presence that compelled Simon Peter to hold up a mirror to himself. He didn't like what he saw, and this brought Simon Peter to his knees:

"Depart from me, Lord, for I am a sinful man." And we know that Simon Peter meant it because, throughout the Gospels, Simon Peter spoke aloud whatever he was thinking in the moment. Transparent to a fault, Simon Peter was often guilty of over-sharing.

Which is really good for us because that openness lets us know Simon Peter better and, in that knowing, gives us an opportunity to know ourselves better, especially how we live our faith. In this passage, for example, Simon Peter shows us how to make a good confession: Simon Peter encounters Jesus, lets Jesus soak in, reflects upon the encounter, is prompted to honestly examine his life, finds it wanting, is sincerely remorseful for his sins, and opens his soul to Jesus on bended knee. Good steps, but what's most important is how Simon Peter took them—honestly, sincerely, openly.

Compare Simon Peter's confession to a bad one. My own. Though it is one I made decades ago, I literally do remember it like it was yesterday. I was a junior in college and, for some unknown reason, one day it occurred to me that I had been treating others poorly. I decided to go to Confession. I recall clearly, however, that I just felt the need to check a box so that I could feel better about myself and move on. It was more calculated than heartfelt.

I arrived at church early so that I could have a good view of the priests as they walked to their confessional booths. I was so embarrassed about what I had to say that I needed to find the perfect priest: mostly deaf, preferably senile. Jackpot. I spotted my man. Hearing aid and very old—I pegged him at 137. As he entered his booth I beelined for his line. I may or may not have bumped a nun out of the way to get to the head of the line. That was no matter to me. I just added it to my sin-list. I wanted a quick, drive-thru confession; say the words, hear that my sins were forgiven, and then bolt from the church.

I knelt in that dark booth and rattled off a list of sins to a face I couldn't see. Finally, I stopped and listened. And then . . . nothing. I knelt in that suffocating silence for the old priest to mutter his words and send me on my way. Had he rewarded himself with a nap? Had he gone on to his eternal reward? Then, it came. "Well," he said, "You're just a BIG IDIOT."

He then went on to explain to me at length why exactly I was acting like a big idiot, including how I lacked contrition as I raced through my laundry list of sins. Only then did I truly have a "Depart from me, Lord, for I am a sinful man" moment. Kneeling became more than gesture, and my admission of sorrow—accompanied by tears—much more genuine.

After his confession, Simon Peter was comforted by Jesus with four words: "Do not be afraid." Jesus gave to Simon Peter what he needed in that moment. Me? Jesus gave me a 137-year-old priest who wasn't afraid to call BS when he smelled it. Exactly what I needed.

{ *The root for the word "sin" is "missing the mark." Alone on a seashore with Jesus, how would you describe to Jesus how you've been missing the mark?*

day thirty

GOOD EXPECTATIONS

(Jesus said:) "A good tree does not bear rotten fruit, nor does
a rotten tree bear good fruit. For every tree is known by its
own fruit. For people do not pick figs from thornbushes, nor
do they gather grapes from brambles. A good person out of
the store of goodness in his heart produces good, but an evil
person out of a store of evil produces evil. . . ."
—Luke 6:43–45

Our diets were originally restricted to fruits and vegetables. God gave humans only plants and fruit to eat (Gen. 1:29). It was not until after Noah and the flood that God included animals on the menu: "Every creature that is alive shall be yours to eat; I give them to you all as I did the green plants" (Gen. 9:3).

Those Genesis passages are about more than dietary instructions. Taken together, they describe God's expectations for us. God had given humans dominion over creatures—we were to care for them in God's place (Gen. 1:26). God trusted us, a trust we betrayed in all that sinning we committed after creation, culminating in the flood. Though made in God's image and "very good," we showed how capable we were of doing very bad things, especially violence. It was with disappointment—and not as a reward—that God relented: "You may eat Bambi."

Despite our capacity for doing bad things, God never took our free will away. But God continues to expect that we will choose to store goodness in our hearts instead of evil. That choice matters. Out of the store of goodness comes goodness, just as evil produces evil. Further, good will never come from bad and bad will never come from good. Thorn bushes cannot produce figs. And, though I have no idea what can be gathered from brambles, Jesus tells us it is definitely not grapes.

We generally don't think of goodness as something that exists in its own right, but St. Thomas Aquinas did: *Bonum est diffusuvum sui.* Goodness tends to spread. Far from being inanimate, it is in the nature of goodness to animate. It wants to move and flow. Further, goodness tends to produce good acts, and those acts, in turn, nourish goodness.

The same goes for evil. While I don't think Aquinas ever said this, it is also true that *"malum est diffusuvum sui."* Evil tends to produce evil acts, and those acts, in turn, nourish evil. As is the case with goodness, there is a symbiosis between those who act badly and the bad itself. Evil feeds and is fed upon.

It is inevitable that good and evil come into conflict as they spread. That is basically what the Book of Revelation is all about: the battle between the forces of light and the forces of darkness. Tolkien captured this conflict in the shadow imagery that runs throughout his *The Lord of the Rings* trilogy. The shadow animates dark acts while the dark acts, in turn, extend the shadow. Light can be overshadowed, but light is also powerful enough to break through darkness. What's more, it is impossible to stand somewhere that is not in either light or shadow. We must choose one or the other, though we often act as though we can just flit about between them.

Light is heaven and shadow is hell. We don't like to talk much about the reality of either, especially hell. This reluctance is something that C. S. Lewis captured in many of his books. In *The Great Divorce*, for example, the dead who live in Grey Town could simply choose to ride a bus to heaven. They don't because they refuse to admit to themselves that hell even exists. C. S. Lewis saw our reduction of hell to pure fiction as a masterful stroke by the master of evil.

But we have drifted too far from fruit. One day Jesus and his disciples were walking down a road. They were very hungry. Jesus saw a fig tree and walked over to it. Jesus expected to see figs on the tree because, in that climate at that time, fig trees were almost constantly with fruit. But this tree had none. Jesus cursed the tree: "May no fruit ever come from you again" (Matt. 21:19). The tree immediately withered.

God is generous in giving us the freedom to choose good or evil, but we shouldn't mistake that generosity for lowered expectations. The choice is clear, as is what God expects from us.

What do you make of this quotation from C. S. Lewis: "There are only two kinds of people in the end: those who say to God, 'Thy will be done,' and those to whom God says, in the end, 'Thy will be done.' All that are in Hell, choose it."[11]

day thirty-one

FIRE IN THE HOLE

"I have come to set the earth on fire, and how I wish it were
already blazing!" **—Luke 12:49**

Jesus lived during an apocalyptic age, and the Gospels—written between 30 to 70 years after his death and resurrection—certainly reflected the first century's fascination with the end times. This passage is apocalyptic. We know that because it is placed at the conclusion of a parable about how servants must remain vigilant because they don't know when their master will return.

There is more to the passage, however, than a teaching about the end times. Jesus was challenging his followers in their own time. I imagine Jesus looking out at faces and seeing bland, milquetoast expressions. He's got a fiery message that, if sincerely heard, should be setting hearts ablaze. Jesus wishes it were already so. There is, however, no spark in these people.

One reason I think the passage is more of a personal challenge than an apocalyptic message is what Jesus said in the preceding verse: "Much will be required of the person entrusted with much, and still more will be demanded of the person entrusted with more." Jesus implored his followers to show some passion, to make the most of what they had.

I was asked recently what the biggest problem our young people today are facing. I think it is drifting, meandering along without direction. One very disturbing symptom is the escalating suicide rates among those in their 20s and 30s. It used to be that those in their 50s and 60s represented the highest suicide group, perhaps a sign of mid-life crisis. Now it's a young-life crisis; that age group leads this very undesirable category.

There are likely many reasons for this shift, but I suspect it's rooted in increased isolation (partly due to overuse of personal technology), decreased community (the "bowling alone" phenomenon), and the absence of faith life in the lives of young people. That's another shocking statistic: Church attendance among younger generations is at the all-time low of 20 percent. Even more, 60 percent of those who grew up going to church no longer do so. Taken together, increased isolation and decreased community, especially faith community, arc cancerous for a culture. The cure can be found in more purposeful living.

Where do we get purpose from? It is not from endless navel-gazing and focus on self-interest. Purpose comes from moving outside ourselves toward others. It also comes from recognizing a reality that exists below the surface of daily living, something deeper than the stuff we trudge through every day. So, it really is important to lift eyes off cellphones and into those of another, just as it is to practice faith within a faith community.

That's what Jesus was saying to his followers in the "set the earth on fire" passage: The Kingdom is here with you now—GET MOVING! Jesus is here with us now with the same message: There's essential work to be done—feeding the hungry, fighting for racial justice, sheltering the homeless, educating the marginalized, healing the sick, nurturing our planet, protecting the vulnerable, building up community. Play big, not small. God calls each of us to do something. Together.

Want a sign? Look for what is blazing. Fire changes everything around us, including ourselves. It reshapes landscapes. We should be on fire watch, ever vigilant. If we're not, we are going to just sleep-walk past burning bushes. Yes, we'll be safe from getting burned, but Jesus reminds us that we're not called to live safe lives. Look up! Fires abound.

I wonder how long that bush burned in that ancient desert without being seen until Moses came along and, unlike everyone else who had come along, looked up instead of casting his eyes down. Even more, Moses put aside what he had been doing (perhaps what he was stuck in) and climbed that mountain so that he could see that fire up close. He approached the fire and perceived God within it. In that vision, Moses knew his former life had been burned away. From that encounter with flame came purpose. Moses stopped drifting and started living.

> Earth's crammed with heaven,
> And every bush afire with God,
> But only he who sees takes off his shoes;
> The rest sit round and pluck blackberries.
> **—Elizabeth Barrett Browning**

{ *Where is there a burning bush? Will its flames singe, or would you rather water it down?*

day thirty-two
MESSIANIC SECRET

Many of the Samaritans of that town began to believe in him
because of the word of the woman who testified, "He told me
everything I have done." —John 4:39

I f I could perform miracles, I would spend a lot of time telling
people about it. That would be yet another way that I am not
much like Jesus. When Jesus performed a miracle, he often
instructed the healed person to tell no one.

Some biblical scholars in the twentieth century fixated on the
"tell no one" instruction (especially as found in the Gospel of
Mark) and came to call it the "Messianic Secret." There are various
theories about why Jesus was so adamant that his miracles be
kept under wraps, but the most likely one is that he was trying
to counter popular messianic expectations. The Jewish people
under Roman occupation yearned for the Messiah, the "Anointed
One" (in Greek, "Christ"). Kings were anointed, so the title was
a reference to a kingly savior, a powerful ruler along the lines
of King David. Miracle working would tend to reinforce that
Messiah stereotype, a type that didn't fit Jesus.

That is a plausible explanation for the Messianic Secret.
But I think that Jesus's efforts to dampen enthusiasm for his
miracles was about more than that: miracles elicited an emotional

response, and emotion does not ground us in deep faith. I rely upon an unconventional theologian for this interpretation— Flannery O'Connor:

> There is a question whether faith can or is supposed to be emotionally satisfying. I must say that the thought of everyone lolling about in an emotionally satisfying faith is repugnant to me. I believe we are ultimately directed Godward but that this journey is often impeded by emotion.[12]

The miracles Jesus performed must have been highly charged with emotion, often followed by shouts of "I believe!" There's no reason to doubt the sincerity of these confessions of faith, but one wonders how long they lasted. Jesus likely saw miracles as an invitation to would-be believers, but only that. Faith had to be in Jesus and his message, not in the miracles he performed.

We repeatedly see in the Gospels how the words of Jesus satisfied a hunger people didn't know they had. Tasting Jesus's words internally led to visceral faith, one that sank in more deeply than an emotional response. Look at the parables. Chewing on those strange, perplexing teachings must have churned up something inside.

Imagine, for example, the facial expressions of the crowd as Jesus described the Kingdom. They would have expected Jesus to draw from tradition and compare it to the mighty cedar of Lebanon. Jesus instead compared the Kingdom to the mustard seed, a troublesome plant that was so invasive that Jewish teachings prohibited it from gardens. Similarly, Jesus taught that the Kingdom was like leaven (a putrid, corrupted substance), and a banquet hall filled with only the poor, blind, and lame (society's untouchables). Jesus refused to serve up the standard fare, and that must have left his listeners slack-jawed. Who is this man and what is he saying? Jesus's words rendered his audiences confused, troubled, and . . . fully engaged.

Nowhere is the transformative power of the Jesus-effect captured better than in John's description of the encounter with the Samaritan woman at the well. As a Samaritan, she was reviled by the Jews. As an outcast among her own people, she was forced to go to the well at noon instead of early morning with the respectable women. Yet, this woman emerged as one of the great disciples in the Gospels, all due to a single conversation with Jesus.

They bantered back and forth, just the two of them. The woman challenged Jesus, and Jesus did the same to her. It seems that the conversation was a lengthy one and, by the end of it, the words of Jesus had brought wholeness to a fractured life, faith emerging from a deeper understanding of self. When the disciples returned to the scene, they found Jesus and the woman so engrossed in conversation that they were reduced to silence. But the woman was not. She raced into town and told everyone about Jesus. The townspeople came to believe in Jesus simply because of words spoken by this outcast woman.

We do not know the name of this woman, yet her faith made her one of the earliest and most successful missionaries in Christianity—all because of an encounter with the words and person of Jesus. No miracle required.

Simply being with Jesus can make us whole; it's a relationship that leads to an interior sense of connectivity that transcends emotion. What do you make of this teaching by Julian of Norwich: "Faith is nothing but a right understanding of our being."

day thirty-three
I SEE DEAD PEOPLE

"I am going to prepare a place for you ... so that where I am
you also may be." **—John 14:2-3**

O ne of the strange and beautiful things about being Catholic
is connecting to the dead. All Saints Day. All Souls Day.
November is even set aside as "Pray for the Dead" month. It
is probably strange for those on the outside looking in, but, to
Catholics anyway, it makes a lot of sense.

That morbidity may be a culturally Catholic thing. But what is
true for all Christian faiths is something much deeper: the belief
that our lives are changed—not ended—when we die. *Vita mutator,*
non tollitur. That belief is outside what we can know with our
senses, but that doesn't make it nonsense. And I think that we
all possess a kind of sixth sense in knowing this. Deep down we
know that there is more to us than just our bodies, and that there
is more to this world than what our eyes can see. We also know
that this is all somehow connected. We feel that to be true in
random, other-worldly moments. The Irish describe the place of
that encounter as the "thin space."

That means that bonds formed between souls in life are not
severed when one soul moves on from here to there. I still, for
example, talk to my dad, even though he died many years ago.

The way I talk to him is different, as is the way I hear him. But the conversation still happens. That's why praying for and talking with the dead matters. Connecting in the thin space keeps us bonded to the ones we love who have passed. Gabriel Garcia Marquez captured the feel of this in *One Hundred Years of Solitude.* The dead just keep popping up throughout the novel, in what the literary world calls magical realism. The mystical becomes mundane; the supernatural feels natural.

Praying for the dead, however, is not just about connecting with those whose lives have changed. It also has a lot to do with how we live the lives we are living now. I am reminded of that at funerals.

I go to a lot of funerals. Yes, they can be very painful, especially when a young person has died. But mostly they are a blessing, even (strangely) an opportunity. If I listen closely to how loved ones pray for and talk about departed ones, I learn a lot about how I can live my own life better. The columnist David Brooks wrote that it is much more important to live "eulogy lives" than "resume lives."[13] Nothing brings the truth of that home more than really listening to eulogies.

That's especially true at funerals when the voice of the one who has left is heard so clearly in the voices of the living. A departed parent, for example, often speaks through the voices of her children. In those voices I often find myself hearing how to be a better parent—the importance of being a eulogy father.

I even hear those voices in prayer cards that are given out at funerals, especially if they include the departed loved one's own words. Here is a dad's voice in words to his children on his prayer card, words that carry a lot of wisdom for all of us: "Let me live in your heart as well as your mind. You can love me most by letting your love reach out to our loved ones by embracing them and living in their love. Love does not die, people do."

It's maybe the Irish in me that's drawn to the thin space. Heck, I'm even a regular reader of obituaries (a/k/a "the Irish sport pages"). But I don't think it's just me. We all yearn for that connection, one that deep down we know is there because, even deeper down, we also know that life doesn't ever end.

{ *In* The Great Divorce *by C. S. Lewis, relationships transcend life and death, and this includes sharing excellent advice about how to live better. Imagine being with a departed loved one. What advice would she or he share about eulogy living?*

day thirty-four
FLESHLY PEOPLE

*Brothers, I could not talk to you as spiritual people,
but as fleshly people, as infants in Christ. I fed you
milk, not solid food, because you were unable to take
it. Indeed, you are still not able, even now, for you are
still of the flesh. While there is jealousy and rivalry
among you, are you not of the flesh, and behaving in an
ordinary human way?* **—1 Corinthians 3:1–3**

*Let no one deceive himself. If anyone among you
considers himself wise in this age, let him become a fool
so as to become wise. For the wisdom of this world is
foolishness in the eyes of God.* **—1 Corinthians 3:18–19**

St. Paul believed that there are two kinds of people in this
world: Fleshly types are wise in the ways of the world, and
master it, but are foolish in God's eyes. The other type—spiritual
people—are not foolish in God's eyes but look foolish to everyone
else. Paul didn't see any middle ground between these two types
of people.

Nothing was in the middle for St. Paul. When he went by the
name Saul, he despised Christians so much that he traveled from
town to town to round them up for persecution. Once they were

assembled, Saul tried to knock some orthodoxy into their heads with rocks thrown at high speed. Christians feared for their lives around Saul, and with good reason. Saul probably fed off that fear as a sign that his violent ways were having the intended effect of pushing Christians away from the false prophet Jesus and back into the fold where they belonged.

Jesus, though, had a different way in mind for Saul. Maybe Jesus first tried to get Saul's attention with gentle nudges, signals that should have indicated to Saul that he needed to pump the brakes on all the violence. If so, it never took. Subtlety doesn't work on strident personalities, and Saul was one strident person. Jesus ended up taking the direct approach with Saul: knocking him off his horse with a lightning bolt, blinding Saul in the process. The violence ended, but the strident personality and passion didn't. Saul became Paul and went all in for Jesus.

Paul kept up his travels, but now moved from town to town for Jesus instead of against him. The message took hold in many cities, and Paul gained converts, especially among the gentiles. Paul kept in touch with the Christian communities he founded through letters he wrote to them while traveling about. Many are gentle and affirming, but a lot of them are not. The Corinthians were particularly vexing for Paul. They would often snap back into "behaving in an ordinary human way" even after they'd tasted the spiritual life. They struggled to grasp, for example, that they couldn't get into Jesus while continuing to get into orgies. That is probably the way it is for most of us. Not the orgy part so much, but that sense that we would be more inclined to follow Jesus's way if it were made more our way.

But, that's just not the way it is. Following Jesus—choosing the foolishness that spiritual types embrace—is a "yes" or "no" to God's grace, not a maybe, kinda, sorta. We don't get to soften Jesus so that he goes down easier. And that also means that how we live should look and feel a little different when we are following Jesus than when we are not following Jesus.

WWJD bracelets were popular for a time: "What would Jesus do?" The bracelets have gone out of fashion, but the question shouldn't. What Jesus would want us to do is live more in "righteousness," a word that's even less popular than WWJD bracelets. But that's because we confuse it for "self-righteousness," a not very good word at all. Much better is what Jesus meant when he called his followers to righteous living: moral conduct in conformity with God's will.

It really does matter, as Paul insisted in his letters, how we live. God's will for us is that our faith in Jesus be manifested by how faithfully we live out his example. To live as God would want us to live—especially in our love for each other—is the choice we make when we choose Jesus.

That is likely the first lesson Paul learned when he was knocked off his horse by that lightning bolt and was blinded. Immediately converted from powerful to powerless, Paul encountered what living spiritually meant in the love that was shown to him by people who should have hated him for what he had done. That, after all, is what the wisdom of the world would call for. God, though, calls that kind of wisdom foolishness. In his blindness, Paul came to see it that way too.

{ *What would Jesus want me to see about myself if I were struck blind by a lightning bolt?*

day thirty-five
PRUNING

*For we are (God's) handiwork, created in Christ Jesus
for the good works that God has prepared in advance,
that we should live in them.*
—Ephesians 2:10

I like to read local newspapers when I travel. Once while doing this in a small town I came across an article about a seventh-grade basketball tournament. It was gratifying to see kids' games being covered, something wholesome and pure. I scanned the team names: Coyotes. Hoop Dreams. Panthers. NO MERCY FOR FAILURE.

That last one didn't seem to fit. I imagined what it must have been like playing for the coach of that team. Kid gets scored on; failure—no mercy. Kid misses a shot; failure—no mercy. Team loses; all the kids are failures—no mercy for any of them. Show enough failure and you're likely shown the door.

This got me to wondering if the coach was a John Kreese disciple. Remember John Kreese? He was the sensei of Cobra Kai in the movie *Karate Kid*. Kreese was certainly a "no mercy for failure" kind of guy, as evidenced by the dojo's motto: "Strike First. Strike Hard. NO MERCY." He pounded that teaching into the students in his dojo. Most of the movie is about Cobra Kai kids showing no mercy to other kids, especially the loner-loser, Danny.

Danny found a much different sensei to teach karate to him. Mr. Myagi was patient, understanding, and . . . merciful. He used karate for self-defense and agreed to teach it to Danny only when Danny promised to use it in the same way.

Mr. Myagi's methods were unorthodox: Danny had to repeatedly wax cars in a particular manner—a circular "wax on, wax off" motion. He was required to paint a fence in a specific manner as well, constantly bending his wrist up and down. Same kind of drill for sanding the floor. Danny didn't understand any of it. Until, that is, he started to practice karate and realized that the specific, repeated motions had prepared him for the moves that would bring success.

It wasn't just karate moves, however, that were taking hold inside Danny. He was being shaped by Mr. Myagi; the repeated "wax on, wax off" of ethical actions, kindness, and patience were becoming habits for him. Danny entrusted to Mr. Myagi his formation as both a karate competitor and as a human being, and that trust was rewarded abundantly.

"There are very few . . . who realize what God would make of them if they abandoned themselves entirely to His hands and let themselves be formed by His grace" (St. Ignatius of Loyola). God—the Supreme Sensei—asks of us: "Trust in me; let me shape you." In the second Genesis creation story, God got down into the soil ("adamah" in Hebrew) and created the human (Adam), even breathing the breath of life into his lips. The intimacy of that creation lives on in our creation. God's hands continue to work the clay, getting us in shape. "For we are," as St. Paul wrote to the Ephesians, "God's handiwork."

Even more, our hands join God's hands in continuing the work of creation. Since we are made in God's image, we carry within us an impression of the divine. We are not to keep this gift to ourselves; we are called to work the clay to impress God's shape upon creation.

There was an intimate, reverential scene in *Karate Kid*[14] that captured how we, God's handiwork, can lend our hands to this essential work. Danny came upon Mr. Myagi while he was quietly, patiently pruning a bonsai tree. Mr. Myagi asked Danny to take hold of small scissors and join him in pruning the little tree. Danny, afraid of damaging the bonsai, politely declined the invitation. Danny eventually agreed to join in the pruning only after Mr. Myagi offered reassurance: "Close eyes. Trust. Concentrate. Think only tree . . . nothing exists in all the world but tree." "How will I know if I am doing it right?" Danny asked. "You know if picture is the right one if it comes from inside you," said the sensei.

{ *Who in my life has shaped or is shaping me? In what ways can I continue to labor with God in continuing the act of creation?*

day thirty-six
LUKEWARM LIVING

"I know your works; I know that you are neither cold nor hot. I wish you were either cold or hot. So, because you are lukewarm, neither hot nor cold, I will spit you out of my mouth." —**Revelation 3:15–16**

The most common question I ask my students in Scripture class: "What's the literary form?" Young people—like a lot of people who read the Bible—often fail to recognize that the Bible is a book of many different books. That is, as with any library, there is a constellation of literary forms within the Bible. Ignoring this inevitably leads to misunderstanding. No one, for example, would read poetry the same way that a history textbook is read. The same is true for reading Psalms (poetry meant to be sung) and Chronicles (faith history). Different literary forms, different ways to read and understand them.

The most misread book in the Bible is Revelation. Many mistakenly read it as a hidden prophecy reserved for some distant future age. That's not so at all. Revelation was thoroughly grounded in the time within which it was written—the late first-century persecution of Christians by the Romans. It does point toward the future, but it is mostly a message of hope for those early Christians during the hard time they were living in. The author—

John the apostle (also known as John of Patmos)—encouraged his Christian community to remain faithful, and to be assured that good will triumph over evil.

This assurance is given through the use of a literary form called "apocalyptic," a popular genre 2,000 years ago that is not commonly used today. This form is characterized by highly symbolic imagery, and those early Christians knew exactly what John's symbols represented. They knew, for example, that the beastly 666 was not about a future egomaniacal, destructive despot. It was a reference to the egomaniacal, destructive despot who was persecuting them during their own time—Emperor Nero.

Simply transposing the imagery from that time to our time doesn't work. What does work is a two-step method that is useful whenever we read the Bible: First, what message did the authors intend to convey? (The authors being God and the human writers inspired by God.) Second, what is the message for me? Taking the time to answer that first question by examining the literary form and the historical context helps us answer that second question. It turns out that Revelation, when unlocked in this way, does hold meaning for us. The "spit out the lukewarm" passage is a great example.

John targeted his "spitting out" at the people of Laodicea. His description of the lukewarm water there would have been readily recognized by the Laodiceans and the surrounding communities. Laodicea was known for having terrible water that could even make its residents sick. As a wealthy city, Laodicea certainly had the resources to build a better water system. Apparently, it didn't upgrade the system because the bad water was good for its thriving textile industry. So, the Laodiceans settled for bad water so that they could make more money.

The quality of water was much better in two nearby cities. One was known for its hot springs—medicinal waters famous for treating maladies. The residents of another nearby city, located at the foot of a mountain, drank cold, clear water. The quality of living in those days, much like in our day, depended upon the quality of water. Neither of those two cities would settle for lukewarm, smelly, sometimes sickening water, the way that Laodicea did.

We know a lot about those water supplies because of archeology, and that, in turn, tells us a lot about the inhabitants of those cities—especially the Laodiceans, who settled for a reduced quality of life so that they could have more stuff. I sometimes wonder what archeological sites 2,000 years from now would reveal about Americans today. Let's say, for example, that a dig uncovered a massive warehouse that had lettering across the side, "Amazon Fulfillment Center." Think of all the stuff that archeologists might find within that warehouse. What would they conclude about what it took to fulfill us?

But John of Patmos was doing more than just questioning the value judgments being made by the Laodiceans with his "I spit out the lukewarm" challenge. It's also a reference to the living water that is Jesus Christ, and the unwillingness of the Laodiceans to drink fully from that water. That is, while they heard the message, they kept on living lukewarm lives, mired in a malaise of their own making. What they did with their water they also did with their relationship with Jesus. They settled.

There is a terrific line in the famous prayer *Anima Christi* (Soul of Christ): "Blood of Christ, inebriate me." Some years ago, I picked up a translation of this prayer and "inebriate" had been changed to "influence." That tepid translation feels so Laodicean.

The verb used by the anonymous medieval author of the *Anima Christi* is very clear: *Sanguis Christi, inebria me.* Unsettling, even disturbing imagery.

Now, as a school administrator, I'm not one to promote a lot of drunkenness, especially among teens. As a religion teacher, however, I hope inebriation is exactly what happens as young people drink from living water. Being filled up with that water—the kind of water that paradoxically flows from both a hot spring and a cold mountain stream—comes from a very different kind of fulfillment center.

{ *Where in my life do I settle for lukewarm water? Where might living water be found?*

day thirty-seven
THE FIRST STREAKER

*Now a young man followed him wearing nothing but a linen
cloth about his body. They seized him, but he left the cloth
behind and ran off naked.* —**Mark 14:51-52**

There are two different conclusions to the Gospel of Mark—
"Shorter Ending" and "Longer Ending"—both of unknown
origin. What is known is that the last words written in Mark's
hand concern the women who discovered the empty tomb: "Then
they went out and fled from the tomb, seized with trembling and
bewilderment. They said nothing to anyone, for they were afraid"
(Mk. 16:8).

"Afraid." That's a fitting word to end Mark's account, the rawest
and most visceral of the four. Fear is a theme that runs throughout,
as is abandonment of Jesus at his time of greatest need.

Most of the disciples fled from Jesus in the Garden of
Gethsemane. Jesus had gone off to pray, asking only that Peter,
James, and John stay awake. It is here that Jesus pleaded with
his Abba (Aramaic for "father," conveying intimacy) to "take this
cup away from me, but not what I will but what you will." Utterly
spent, Jesus returned to his closest companions, only to find them
asleep. That's when Judas arrived with the chief priests, scribes,
and an angry mob. Judas kissed Jesus, swords were drawn, an

ear was cut off a servant, and Jesus was arrested. Chaos was followed by panic. "And they all left him and fled."

The scene then shifted to the trial before the Sanhedrin. It is here that the only disciple who had remained at least on the periphery of Jesus was confronted by some threatening bystanders. It happened in the courtyard outside, and Peter, overwhelmed by fear, denied Jesus three times.

It is between the arrest at Gethsemane and the trial before the Sanhedrin that Mark included a most curious reference—the young man seized by the mob who ran away naked. It is such a strange, awkward insertion; it just doesn't fit within the flow of the high drama of the narrative. A few years ago, it hit me: Mark included the naked youth reference because that naked youth was Mark.

I was quite proud of my theory until I then looked at biblical commentaries and discovered that theologians have been speculating for centuries that Mark was the naked youth. It does make sense. Mark's Gospel is the only one that included this snippet. It reads as if the author were lending credibility to his account as a firsthand witness—"I was there when it happened!" Also, given that the Crucifixion took place around AD 30 and Mark wrote his Gospel between 30 and 40 years later, it is certainly possible that the naked youth and Mark the evangelist were one and the same.

What is more interesting, however, is to ponder what was going through Mark's mind as he wrote about the arrest of Jesus, at least three decades after it happened. Now an older man, Mark had lived most of his life grappling with the memory that he had abandoned Jesus in the Garden. Perhaps, that is why Mark wrote so glowingly about those who didn't abandon Jesus:

There was Joseph of Arimathea, who "courageously went to Pilate and asked for the body of Jesus" (Mk. 15:43). And also the courageous women—Mary, Mary Magdalene, and Salome—who stayed near Jesus throughout his suffering, death, and burial. If discipleship means steadfastness during those times when it is a challenge to remain with Jesus, those women were the only ones who passed the test. Maybe Mark pictured the women at the Cross while he wrote, wishing that his younger self had also chosen to stand there.

It is also believed that Mark served as an interpreter to Peter during his travels. If so, that relationship must have influenced Mark and what he wrote in his Gospel. I imagine the conversations that Peter and Mark must have had with each other, both describing how they had abandoned Jesus during his time of trial, Peter three times in the courtyard and Mark in the Garden. Maybe Peter helped the younger Mark come to terms with the betrayal.

For both men, abandoning Jesus did not sever their relationship with Jesus. A new Peter emerged from that betrayal: a life lived in steadfast devotion to Jesus. The same was true for that naked youth who had fled in fear. Yes, discipleship means staying with Jesus during the hard times, but it also means that Jesus wants to reconcile with us when we don't. That's the good news Mark brought to his Gospel from firsthand experience.

Ever abandon anyone during a time of need, or get abandoned yourself? If so, is there room for reconciliation?

day thirty-eight
QUID EST VERITAS

So Pilate said to him, "Then you are a king?" Jesus answered,
"You say I am a king. For this I was born and for this I came
into the world, to testify to the truth. Everyone who belongs
to the truth listens to my voice." Pilate said to him,
"What is truth?" —**John 18:37–38**

A friend of mine who knows I've taught Scripture for many years asked me, "Why is Pontius Pilate singled out in the Apostles' Creed?" Great question. I hope someday he finds someone smart enough to give him the answer.

All I have is a theory. From the very beginning, Christians have been fascinated by Pilate because it is so hard to understand why he allowed himself to do what he did. Pilate seemed to believe that Jesus was an innocent man, yet he still had him tortured and killed. Wondering about that makes us wonder about ourselves: Are we also capable of readily separating what we believe on the inside from what we do on the outside?

We are if we are like Pilate. He was missing that first part—truly believing on the inside with conviction. That inner emptiness left Pilate adrift without an anchor; he had no transcendent truth to guide his decisions. We know this about Pilate because of the question he asked Jesus: *Quid est veritas?* What is truth? It was one of those not-really-a-question questions. What Pilate was really

120

saying was that there is no truth. Period. Completely unmoored, Pilate was free to make things up as he went along and do whatever suited him best in the moment.

Sophomores who have entered my Scripture class over the years have never worn *quid est veritas* shirts. They never had to—most sophomores live it. It's one of the reasons I have always enjoyed teaching them. I like their scrappy "I will not let adults insert their truth for my truth" take on life. For sophomores, asserting independence means rejecting commonly held beliefs. The wiser ones, however, realize that today it takes greater independence to hold that truth does exist than to join the herd in believing that it doesn't. Those wiser ones also come to understand that the reality of truth is not negated simply because it is sometimes difficult to discover. Being human requires living with our limitations, and our inability to discern truth always and everywhere is one of them.

So, yes, we live in *quid est veritas* times. How did we get here? There's likely no single reason, but there is a good example that offers a clue.

Harvard's original seal, adopted in 1692, included the words "Christ" and "Church" and three open books: the top two books were face-up; the bottom book faced down. The face-up books represented what could be learned through reason. The face-down book symbolized that not all could be known that way: truth must also be discovered outside human reason through God's revelation.

When Harvard dropped faith and became secular it also dropped Christian references from its seal. "Christ" and "Church" were removed; only "Veritas" (Truth) remains. Even more interesting, however, was that the face-down book was turned up.

No need to look to God for revelation—humans have access to all that needs to be known through reason. Truth—if there even is such a thing—can only be created between our ears.

I am not singling out Harvard here. I share this example only because it is illustrative of a phenomenon that has accompanied our culture's shift to the post-Christian era. I am also not minimizing reason, nor the importance of data and science; all are needed now more than ever given the challenges we face. We can learn much from those books turned up.

We reduce ourselves to a very puny people, however, when we forget that truth can be discovered through faith in addition to reason, both being gifts from God. We also reduce our humanity when we deny that there are basic truths that should guide our decisions. As I ask students who insist that there is only "their" truth, not "the" truth, and that truth is whatever individuals determine to be true: "Oh, so Hitler could have been right after all?"

What does *quid est veritas* living look like? We return to Pilate and that courtyard for a glimpse. Pilate, certain only that truth can never be found (even though Truth stood before him!), defaulted to the crowd to create it for him. And then he washed his hands.

{ *Is there a transcendent truth around which you have wrapped your life?*

day thirty-nine
EUCHARIST

Whoever eats my flesh and drinks my blood has eternal life, and I will raise him on the last day. For my flesh is true food, and my blood is true drink. **—John 6:54–55**

When did Jesus die? This is a tricky question, but I like to ask my Scripture students anyway. I provide a clue: Find the timing of Passover in the Synoptic Gospels (Matthew, Mark, and Luke) compared to where it is found in the Gospel of John.

In the Synoptic Gospels, the Last Supper was celebrated as the Passover meal, and Jesus was crucified after that. In the Gospel of John, however, Jesus was crucified on the Preparation Day for Passover, the time when lambs throughout Jerusalem were being slaughtered. That means that in John's Gospel, Jesus didn't celebrate the Passover meal. Jesus *was* the Passover meal.

Though a difficult image, it is a necessary one. It harkens back to Exodus, the first Passover that sets the context for the Passion of Christ. In the Exodus story, lambs were sacrificed, and their blood was applied to doorposts so that the angel of death would pass over. The roasted meat was then eaten to fortify the Israelites for their escape from slavery. Thus, the lamb both saved the Israelites from death and nourished them for their journey from slavery to freedom.

Jesus did the same for all of us when he sacrificed himself and rose from the dead. He bore our sins when he was lifted on the cross, and his blood washed those sins away, freeing humanity from its spiritual enslavement. "Lamb of God, you take away the sin of the world . . ." The body of Jesus serves as nourishment for life's journey, a journey that doesn't end when earthly life does. The angel of death passes over.

It has been debated over the centuries if any of this makes logical sense or if it is mostly nonsense. Tertullian said in the third century, "It is certain because it is absurd." That is, the truth of the Crucifixion and Resurrection is credible because it is so incredible. While that is a compelling argument, what is more persuasive to me is how fervently the early Christians believed all this to be true. The testimonies read with complete conviction, including the certainty that the Risen Christ was present in the Eucharist.

The Eucharist was central to early Christian faith, as reflected in a key post-Resurrection narrative: Two disciples encountered a stranger while traveling along the road to Emmaus. It was only at the meal they later shared that they came to see the man was Jesus—they recognized him in "the breaking of the bread" (Lk. 24:13–35). Similarly, the Acts of the Apostles and Epistles include descriptions of the Eucharist as fundamental to Christian worship. The Eucharist was also featured in the first Christian art (on the walls of catacombs) and in the earliest attacks on Christianity (the Romans roused hatred against Christians by characterizing their meals as cannibalism).

Eucharistic meals called to mind the Last Supper for the faithful, but never were they simply re-enactments. The "eats my flesh" passage from John's Gospel is telling. The Greek verb used for "eats" here was not the customary one used for human eating. Rather, it was the Greek word for animal eating, more like "gnaw." The intent is clear: The flesh is true food; the Eucharist is not a mere representation of Jesus. That's what the early Christians believed. Do we?

There are a lot of reasons why Flannery O'Connor should be beatified. Here's one of them, her recounting of a dinner party conversation:

> Mrs. Broadwater said when she was a child and received the Host, she thought of it as the Holy Ghost, He being the "most portable" person of the Trinity; now she thought of it as a symbol and implied that it was a pretty good one. I then said in a very shaky voice, "Well, if it's a symbol, to hell with it."[15]

Jesus lifted bread and told the apostles, "This is my body." Then he held up a cup and said, "This is my blood." Not as pretty good symbols or a swell thing to do for humanity, but as true food and true drink. The root of "Eucharist" is "thanksgiving." There is much to be thankful for.

> *What do you make of this description of the Eucharist by another rightful beatification candidate, C. S. Lewis: "God never meant for man to be a purely spiritual creature. That is why He uses material things like bread and wine to put the new life into us. We may think this rather crude and unspiritual. God does not: He invented eating. He likes matter. He invented it."[16]*

day forty
LIFTING

*When he had said this, as they were looking on, he was lifted
up, and a cloud took him from their sight.*
—Acts of the Apostles 1:9

Like most of 1970s America, I was captivated by the television
mini-series *Roots*. In one of the most moving scenes, Kunta
Kinte (played by John Amos), in the tradition of his forefathers,
lifted his newborn child to a silent, star-filled sky and proclaimed,
"Behold the only thing greater than yourself!" I was so inspired
by this scene that, many years later, I did the same with our
newborns. Perhaps not my best parenting decision—especially
since one of those lifts happened during a Wisconsin winter—but
it did give me a taste of what was to come.

Good parenting requires a lot of lifting. There are thousands
of lifts in and out of car seats, lifts into the air when returning
from work, and lifts onto shoulders after fantastic games. Then
there are the times when spirits need lifting—after not so fantastic
games, bicycle falls, and the loss of a beloved grandparent. Lifting
is what loving parents do.

Which should make us wonder: how loving a parent is God?
Look, for example, at how forsaken his son felt when he was on
the cross. Bystanders said, "He trusted in God; let him deliver

him now if he wants him" (Matt. 27:43). Jesus was left hanging there—God didn't seem to want him.

God doesn't seem to want us sometimes too, and that is most keenly felt when we could really use a lift. We hold up our arms to God and then . . . nothing. That's when God feels more like an absentee parent than a loving one, the kind that disappears when the kids are in greatest need. It could be, however, that the problem resides more with us than with God. That is, our definition of lifting may be too constricted. Just as God's ways are not our ways, so too God's way of lifting is not necessarily our way of lifting.

My older sister, Robin, had cerebral palsy. She fell down a lot, and it was especially painful to watch because she couldn't break her fall. I recall a time when, while playing in our yard, Robin fell very hard. Right after she hit the ground I looked to our mother, who had been at the screen door watching us while we played. She pushed the door open, appeared to be stepping out, and then pulled back behind the door. My mother had a pained expression on her face as she watched Robin pick herself up.

That image of my mother remains for me an image of God. My mother's hands were at the ready. She wanted to pick up Robin out of love. She let Robin pick herself up out of greater love. Deciding when it is best to lift and when it is not is a question that loving parents struggle with. I believe that God struggles in the same way. God's hands are also at the ready. Sometimes it is best that they are not used; other times it is best that they are. Always, though, the decision is made from love.

Here is another image of God: Many years ago, a young man I knew visited his doctor and was told that he had a very aggressive cancer. Most of us would be tremendously upset and fearful upon hearing such news. So was this man, but his most anxious, fear-filled thought was, "How am I going to tell my father?"

His father was stern and demanding, a big man accustomed to getting his way. The young man thought himself to be a failure in his father's eyes. He wasn't going into the family business; he was going into the Jesuits. He perceived this—and other decisions he had made—to have been disappointments to his father. He dreaded his father's reaction to the news of his cancer, as if this too would be a sign of failure.

The young man mustered the courage to go to his father's office and then broke the bad news. He waited for a reaction from his father. Nothing. This was worse than the young man thought it would be. Finally, in silence the father walked over to the son, pulled him into his powerful arms, and just held him. Then the son realized that his father had slowly lifted him off his feet. And the father just held him there.

As a child I thought of the Ascension as Jesus propelling himself into heaven, a kind of holy hovercraft. That's not what happened. God the Father could wait no longer for the return of his son. The Father reached down, took hold of his child, and lifted him up.

{ *When have you felt God lifting you up in a loving embrace?*

Acknowledgments

I am deeply grateful for all those who so generously helped move this book of reflections from concept to completion. First and foremost, I thank my insightful and wise spouse, Terry, for offering such thoughtful feedback as I wrote these reflections over the last couple of years. Thanks also to our children—Hannah, Eddie, and Sam—for their patience over an even greater number of years as they endured my telling of the stories I shared in these reflections.

I am fortunate to be friends with two exceptional English language scholars, Kathy and Greg Meuler. They proofread and edited chapters individually and then collaborated in providing unified guidance to me on content and style. All this they did for the cost of a dinner at Bobby's in Milwaukee, that "Great Place, Good Times" bar and grill.

While every chapter was written with inclusion in this book in mind, most of the Scripture-specific content was culled from lesson plans I created for my classes over the years. That content came from a rich diversity of resources—books, documentaries, homilies, articles, lectures, commentaries, and conversations. The resource I relied upon most, however, was certainly the New American Bible, especially its footnotes. I am so thankful to the writers and editors of the NAB. They created the perfect Bible for the high school religion teacher.

Three mentors shaped my understanding of Scripture and how it can connect with our lives: Dr. John J. Schmitt, Professor of Theology at Marquette University, awakened within me a fascination with Hebrew Scripture. I had planned to become a history teacher; Dr. Schmitt changed those plans. I am also thankful to my spiritual guide, Fr. Frank Majka, sj. Fr. Frank always taught that stories were included in the Bible not because they were so out-of-the-ordinary, but because they came from the ordinary. I have been so fortunate to benefit from Fr. Frank's brilliance: his ability to make complex material accessible to not-so-brilliant people like me. Finally, I am also thankful to our Parish priest at Our Lady of the Lake in Seattle, Fr. Timothy Clark. Soaking in Fr. Tim homilies over the years has been nothing short of life changing. I have never encountered anyone so blessed with the ability to prayerfully peel back layers of Scripture to reveal the meaning of the Word.

Let me also please thank the good people of Paraclete Press for taking a risk with an unknown author. I am especially grateful to its Publisher, Jon Sweeney, for bringing focus and shape to this book.

Finally, I am grateful to the students I taught over the years at Notre Dame High School in north Chicago, Marquette High in Milwaukee, Bishop Blanchet in Seattle, and Seattle Preparatory School. I have come to see more clearly what most teachers realize as they enter the twilight of their careers—you have indeed taught me more than I ever taught you.

Notes

1 A. J. Jacobs, The Year of Living Biblically (New York: Simon and Schuster, 2007).
2 Unforgiven, Malpaso Productions, distributed by Warner Bros., 1992.
3 Parenthood, Imagine Entertainment, distributed by Universal Pictures, 1989.
4 C. S. Lewis, The Voyage of the Dawn Treader (London: Geoffrey Bles, 1952).
5 Flannery O'Connor, The Habit of Being: Letters of Flannery O'Connor, (New York: Farrar, Straus and Giroux, 1979).
6 Flannery O'Connor, "The Fiction Writer and his Country" as found in Mystery and Manners: Occasional Prose, Edited by Sally and Robert Fitzgerald (New York: Farrar, Straus and Giroux, 1969).
7 Flannery O'Connor, A Good Man is Hard to Find (New York: Harcourt, Brace and Company, 1955).
8 Flannery O'Connor, The Habit of Being: Letters of Flannery O'Connor (New York: Farrar, Straus and Giroux, 1979), 373.
9 Flannery O'Connor, A Good Man is Hard to Find.
10 Flannery O'Connor, The Habit of Being, 350.
11 C. S. Lewis, The Great Divorce (New York: HarperCollins Publishers, 1946), 75.
12 Flannery O'Connor, The Habit of Being, 100.
13 David Brooks, Tedtalk, March 2014.
14 Karate Kid, Jerry Weintraub Productions, Distributed by Columbia Pictures, 1984.
15 Flannery O'Connor, The Habit of Being, 125.
16 C. S. Lewis, Mere Christianity (New York: HarperCollins Publishers (US edition), 1952).

About Paraclete Press

WHO WE ARE

As the publishing arm of the Community of Jesus, Paraclete Press presents a full expression of Christian belief and practice—from Catholic to Evangelical, from Protestant to Orthodox, reflecting the ecumenical charism of the Community and its dedication to sacred music, the fine arts, and the written word. We publish books, recordings, sheet music, and video/DVDs that nourish the vibrant life of the church and its people.

WHAT WE ARE DOING

BOOKS | PARACLETE PRESS BOOKS show the richness and depth of what it means to be Christian. While Benedictine spirituality is at the heart of who we are and all that we do, our books reflect the Christian experience across many cultures, time periods, and houses of worship.

We have many series, including *Paraclete Essentials*; *Paraclete Fiction*; *Paraclete Poetry*; *Paraclete Giants*; and for children and adults, *All God's Creatures*, books about animals and faith; and *San Damiano Books*, focusing on Franciscan spirituality. Others include *Voices from the Monastery* (men and women monastics writing about living a spiritual life today), *Active Prayer*, and new for young readers: *The Pope's Cat*. We also specialize in gift books for children on the occasions of Baptism and First Communion, as well as other important times in a child's life, and books that bring creativity and liveliness to any adult spiritual life.

The MOUNT TABOR BOOKS series focuses on the arts and literature as well as liturgical worship and spirituality; it was created in conjunction with the Mount Tabor Ecumenical Centre for Art and Spirituality in Barga, Italy.

MUSIC | PARACLETE PRESS DISTRIBUTES RECORDINGS of the internationally acclaimed choir *Gloriæ Dei Cantores*, the *Gloriæ Dei Cantores Schola*, and the other instrumental artists of the *Arts Empowering Life Foundation*.

PARACLETE PRESS IS THE EXCLUSIVE NORTH AMERICAN DISTRIBUTOR for the Gregorian chant recordings from St. Peter's Abbey in Solesmes, France. Paraclete also carries all of the Solesmes chant publications for Mass and the Divine Office, as well as their academic research publications.

In addition, PARACLETE PRESS SHEET MUSIC publishes the work of today's finest composers of sacred choral music, annually reviewing over 1,000 works and releasing between 40 and 60 works for both choir and organ.

VIDEO | Our video/DVDs offer spiritual help, healing, and biblical guidance for a broad range of life issues including grief and loss, marriage, forgiveness, facing death, understanding suicide, bullying, addictions, Alzheimer's, and Christian formation.

Learn more about us at our website
www.paracletepress.com
or phone us toll-free at 1.800.451.5006

SCAN
TO
READ

You may also be interested in these...

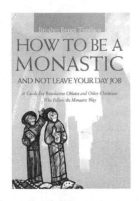
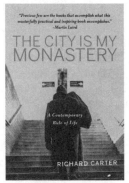